WILDSAM

FIELD GUIDES

Sincere thanks to Tom Kanon at the Tennessee
State Archives and Museum; Nashville Metro Archives;
Nashville Downtown Library; Country Music Hall of Fame;
Vanderbilt University; Rep. Jim Cooper, Alice Randall, John
Egerton, Sidney McAlister, Marshall McKinney, Jennifer Cole,
Jack Sanders, Dave Burden, Hiriam Gates, Jim Hoobler, Rachel
Halvorson; Amy Pastre and Courtney Rowson; Ashley Zeiger
Peak, Margaret Pless, and Eden Walker, for tireless
enthusiasm and wit. And for everything, RWB.

WILDSAM FIELD GUIDES™

A WILDSAM PRESS ORIGINAL,
March 2016

All rights reserved. Published in the
United States by Wildsam Press, New York.
Library of Congress Cataloging-in-Publication
Data have been applied for.

ISBN 978-0-578-11080-6

Book design by Metaleap Creative
Map design by Michael Newhouse

www.wildsam.com

⇛ CONTENTS ⇚

⫸ WELCOME ⫷

WILLIAM EDMONDSON WORKED IN THE OPEN, wearing an apron and cap. He had black-blue skin and he was five-feet-tall. His small bungalow, near Vanderbilt, had a yard cast with throwaway chunks of Nashville limestone that he chiseled with a railroad spike. It is written that Edmondson, a tombstone carver turned folk artist, sometimes drew small audiences, most often his nieces and nephews, who lived nearby. They climbed his peach trees and sat on his sculpted lions, and they watched him. One imagines that he sung, lowly. One also imagines his fine economical touch, his temple vessels swelling, and the rude quarry blocks slowly taking forms. *The New Yorker* wrote about his sculptures' "oddly enchanting eloquence" in 1937, a skepticism unveiled fully when the reviewer later predicted he'd be "soon forgotten."

Truth be told, William Edmondson's story mostly is. That his mother and father were freed slaves. That he was the first black man to win a solo exhibition at New York's MoMA. That his unmarked grave is lost inside the Mount Ararat Cemetery off Elm Hill Pike near a Wendy's and a tire store called Hubcap Heaven.

These subtleties, to me, are what grain histories into heritage.

A city is a commingling of the mundane and the magnificent. The stewing of decades. Nashville, in particular, is flavored by river transients, gospel preachers, southern charmers, Shawnee tribesmen, insurance sellers, lap steel players, biscuit ladies, sorority girls, Jubilee singers, Fugitive poets, and millions more souls who've left their prints behind. It is peppered with moments, like Johnny Cash and Bob Dylan's impromptu studio session in February 1969, or when Andrew Jackson wrote his moonshine letter to Congress, or when the last bison found the salt lick downtown. As the "Music City," I suppose the metaphor of harmony is apropos for this crisscrossed chronology. But when you listen closely, Nashville isn't a place that always makes sense. Cities don't. There are Trails of Tears, Civil Rights protests, rising floods, and those episodes leave indelible markings.

But as Steinbeck wrote, "The world was peopled with wonders." Said another way, William Edmondson found his angels inside limestone blocks. This is how I think of cities. I hope this small book leads towards like-minded discoveries. *-TB*

ESSENTIALS

PUBLICATIONS
Nashville Scene
Tennessean
American Songwriter

ITINERARY
ONE DAY
12 South shopping
City House dinner
Station Inn bluegrass

....

WEEKEND
Country Music Hall of Fame
Broadway honky tonks
Marché brunch
No. 308 cocktails
Natchez Trace drive
Puckett's in Leiper's Fork

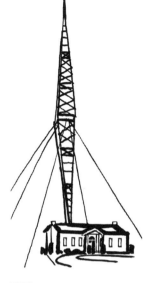

FOODWAY
Hot Chicken
Nashville's cayenne-soaked,
deep fried soul food is tasty
but not for the faint of lip

RADIO
WSM AM 650
Lightning FM 100.1
NPR FM 90.3

RECORD COLLECTION

Harmonica Genius	Deford Bailey
Come On Come On	Mary Chapin Carpenter
Wildwood Flower	The Carter Family
I Walk the Line	Johnny Cash
Barton Hollow	The Civil Wars
The Fabulous Sounds	Flatt & Scruggs
Live	Alison Krauss & Union Station
Satan is Real	The Louvin Brothers
O.C.M.S	Old Crow Medicine Show
Always & Forever	Randy Travis
Revival	Gillian Welch
Alone with His Guitar	Hank Williams

ESSENTIALS

RECENT PROGRESS

- ↪ 1.2-million-square-foot convention center with a four-acre green roof
- ↪ Werthan Lofts and Marathon Motor Works, industrial redesign models
- ↪ Fashion Week, Film Festival spotlighting new creative sectors
- ↪ Mayor's Excellence in Volunteer Engagement certification program
- ↪ $120-million Schermerhorn Symphony adjacent to Country Music Hall
- ↪ Newly opened Parnassus Books, champion of hometown book sellers
- ↪ Start-up support via Jumpstart Foundry, Nashville Entrepreneur Center
- ↪ Detailed Open Space Plan to become greenest city in the South
- ↪ Music Makes Us, a public school curriculum of hip-hop, songwriting, and sound engineering

FUTURE POTENTIAL

- ↪ Utilize Cumberland River for modern use
- ↪ Reinvest in the Fisk neighborhood
- ↪ Focus recruiting on tech companies
- ↪ Establish better public transportation
- ↪ Showcase immigrant communities
- ↪ Redevelop along railroad corridors
- ↪ Secure Major League Soccer franchise
- ↪ Surpass 20,000 downtown residents mark

GREENSPACE

Shelby Bottoms, Beaman Park, Warner Parks, Radnor Lake, Centennial Park, Sevier Park

COLLEGES & UNIVERSITIES

Aquinas, Belmont, Fisk, Lipscomb, Meharry Medical, Nashville State, Tennessee State, Trevecca Nazarene, Watkins College of Art, Vanderbilt

ECONOMY

33%	population [25 and older] with a college degree
5th	fastest-growing U.S. job market, *Bureau of Labor*
3rd	best city for minority entrepreneurs, *Forbes*
174%	downtown population growth since 2000
151,000	new jobs added to economy by 2019

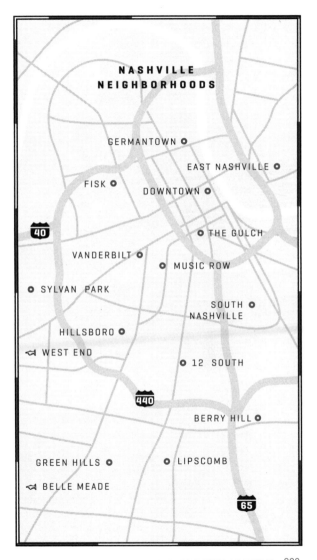

NASHVILLE
NEIGHBORHOODS

GERMANTOWN

EAST NASHVILLE

FISK

DOWNTOWN

40

THE GULCH

VANDERBILT

MUSIC ROW

SYLVAN PARK

SOUTH
NASHVILLE

HILLSBORO

WEST END

12 SOUTH

440

BERRY HILL

GREEN HILLS

LIPSCOMB

BELLE MEADE

65

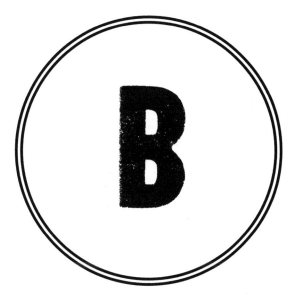

BESTS

A curated list of citywide superlatives including morning coffee, popsicles, taprooms, running trails, drive-ins, haberdashers, guitar repairmen, graphic designers, open mics, and more

≫ FOOD & DRINK ≪

SOUTHERN

City House

1222 4th Ave N
Germantown
cityhousenashville.com

Seasonal menus includes sorghum glazed quail, pulled pork fettuccine, belly ham mozzerella pizza.

....

CAFE

Margot

1017 Woodland St
East Nashville
margotcafe.com

Eighty-seat room in Five Points East with thoughtful French-Italian menu.

....

ITALIAN

Rolf & Daughters

700 Taylor St
Germantown
rolfanddaughters.com

Chef Philip Krajeck's homemade pasta dishes made *Bon Appétit* swoon.

....

MEAT N THREE

Arnold's Country Kitchen

605 8th Ave S
The Gulch
615-256-4455

Southern comforts like fried green tomatoes and 'nana pudding.

....

BURGER

Rotier's

2413 Elliston Pl
Vanderbilt

Greasy Vandy favorite, French bread burgers, family-owned since 1945.

....

HOT CHICKEN

Bolton's Spicy

Chicken and Fish

624 Main St
East Nashville

Fiery fried chicken, white bread, pickles, sweet heaping of ramshackle.

....

BBQ

Martin's BBQ Joint

3108 Belmont Blvd
12 South
martinsbbqjoint.com

Famous for the Redneck taco, 12-hour smoked pork on hoecakes.

....

DELI

Noshville

4014 Hillsboro Cir
noshville.com

Legit Jewish soul food, a la sliced meats sacked six inches high.

FOOD TRUCK

Mas Tacos Por Favor
732 Mcferrin Ave
East Nashville
eatmastacos.com
Former rocker's
Winnebago sells
inventive tacos,
elotes, watermelon
agua fresca.

....

SUPPER CLUB

Twelve at the Table
Citywide
@twelveatthetable
Monthly gourmet
suppers for 12 by art-
ist Evie Coates and
her family.

....

BISCUITS

Loveless Café
8400 TN Hwy 100
Bellevue
lovelesscafe.com
Secret recipe prom-
ises incomparable
fluffiness. Eat with
cheese grits.

....

BRUNCH

Marché
1000 Main St #101
East Nashville
marcheartisanfoods.com
A Parisian vibe
with perfect whiff
of Benton's bacon
and quiche.

POPSICLES

Las Paletas
2911 12th Ave S
12 South
Even in February,
nothing beats an
afternoon pineap-
ple-kiwi ice pop.

....

PEACHES

The Peach Truck
Citywide
thepeachtruck.com
Fresh Georgia
peaches sold with
love by the bag
from an old
Jeep Truck.

....

DONUTS

Fox's Donut Den
3900 Hillsboro Pike
Green Hills
foxsdonutden.com
More unique than
Krispy Kreme,
beloved by Hillsboro
High students next
door.

....

COFFEE

CREMA
15 Hermitage Ave
Downtown
crema-coffee.com
Self-made roasterers
make every espresso
count and teach
classes, too.

SPEAKEASY

Patterson House
1711 Division St
Midtown
thepattersonhouse.com
In-house bitters,
artisan ice chunks,
barmen of the
suspenderred ilk.

....

WINE BAR

Rumours East
1112 Woodland St
East Nashville
rumourseast.com
Victorian digs with
smart wine list, win-
ter fireplace, and a
twinkly-lit backyard.

....

BEER

12 South Taproom
2318 12th Ave S
12 South
12southtaproom.com
Locals pour into
the Hatch-postered
gastropub with
a friendly front
porch.

....

DIVE

Santa's Pub
South Nashville
2225 Bransford Ave
St. Nick-on-a-Harley
kind of spot with $2
beers and awesome
karaoke.

» SHOPPING «

BOOKS

Parnassus

3900 Hillsboro Pike

Green Hills

parnassusbooks.net

Novelist Ann
Patchett co-owns the
well-curated shop.

....

ART SUPPLY

Plaza

633 Middleton St

The Gulch

plazaart.com

Stocks huge selec-
tion and hosts sea-
sonal workshops.

....

MEN'S SHOP

Billy Reid

4015 Hillsboro Pike

Green Hills

billyreid.com

Dapper clothier for
GQ fellas who love
to hunt both mal-
lards and antiques.

HOME GOODS

White's Mercantile

2908 12th Ave S

12 South

whitesmercantile.com

Hank Williams'
granddaughter
Holly curates small
Americana brands.

....

JEANS

Imogene + Willie

2601 12th Ave S

12 South

imogenandwillie.com

Besides designer
denim, I+W throws
Nashville's best
Thursday shindigs.

....

NECKTIES

Otis James

1300 Clinton St

Watkins Park

otisjamesnashville.com

Hand-stitched small
batches of hound-

stooth and plaid,
bowtie and long.

....

THRIFT

Southern Thrift

510 Charlotte Pike

Sylvan Park

southernthriftstore.com

Hand-me-down sets
of china and the best
selection of family
reunion soft tees.

....

ART GALLERY

Rymer

233 Fifth Ave N

Downtown

therymergallery.com

The sprawling space is
the nexus of Art Crawl
held first Saturday of
every month.

....

INSTRUMENTS

Corner Music

2705 12th Ave S

12 South

cornermusic.com
Opened in 1976 minutes from Music Row with specialty in Gibson acoustics.

....

RECORDS

Grimey's New & Preloved Music
1604 8th Ave S
South Nashville
grimeys.com
Top ten vinyl trove in America with tastes from Louvin Brothers to Beastie Boys.

....

TRINKETS

Wonders on Woodland
1110 Woodland St
East Nashville
615-226-5300
Yellow Victorian house of vintage jewelry and assorted collection of thingamajigs.

....

TOYS

Phillips Toy Mart
5207 Harding Pike
Belle Meade
phillipstoymart.com
Lincoln logs, stunt kites, Safari figurines, Lionel train kits.

BICYCLES

East Side Cycles
103 South 11th St
East Nashville
eastside-cycles.com
Five Points center for cyclists, even if renting a cruiser for a day.

....

RUNNING

Athlete's House
1700 Portland Ave
Belmont
athleteshouse.com
Across from Belmont, Tennessee's first running store, circa 1973.

....

KITCHEN WARES

Davis Cookware & Cutlery
1717 21st Ave S
Hillsboro Village
Wizened old pros man the shop with a cast-iron expertise on cooking gear.

....

FLOWERS

Import Flowers
3636 Murphy Rd
Sylvan Park
impfl.com
Dream spot for DIY florists, stocked with a friendly staff.

GROCER

The Turnip Truck
701 Woodland St
East Nashville/Gulch
theturniptruck.com
Preached "organic" and "buy local" before Whole Foods moved in.

....

MEAT & CHEESE

Porter Road Butcher
501 Gallatin Ave
East Nashville
prbutcher.com
Head-to-tail butchers cleave Tennessee's best; in-house cheese expert.

....

WINE

Woodland Wine
1001 Woodland St
East Nashville
615-228-3311
Modern vintner shop with special 6 bottles for $60 deal.

....

TOBACCO

UPTowns Smoke Shop
4001 Hillsboro Pike
Green Hills
uptowns.com
Forbes ranked these cigar aficionados among world's top sellers.

» ACTION «

CINEMA

Belcourt Theatre

2102 Belcourt Ave

belcourt.org

Started with silent movies, hosted Opry in 1936, now a foreign and indie film spot.

....

SYMPHONY

Schermerhorn

1 Symphony Pl

nashvillesymphony.org

Neoclassical concert hall completed in 2006 seats 1,844, 140-show calendar.

....

CONCERT HALL

Ryman Auditorium

116 5th Ave N

ryman.com

Originally a church, the former Opry home is a spiritual experience for all.

MUSEUM

Frist Center for the Visual Arts

919 Broadway

fristcenter.org

Longtime post office building showcases new work every eight weeks.

....

DANCING

The 5 Spot

1006 Forrest Ave

the5spot.club

Monday night 50's soul shakedown, Wednesday night old-time country.

....

BLUEGRASS

Station Inn

402 12th Ave S

stationinn.com

No need to check who's playing. Walk in, buy a beer, tap your foot.

JAZZ

Jazz Cave

1319 Adams St

nashvillejazz.org

BYOB listening room in old Neuhoff meatpacking plant north of Capitol.

....

OPEN MIC

Bluebird Café

4104 Hillsboro Pike

bluebirdcafe.com

Novice songwriters get discovered every Monday night in Green Hills.

....

GOLF

Hermitage Golf Club

3939 Old Hickory Blvd

hermitagegolf.com

Two USGA-rated courses along Cumberland River, open to public.

Percy Warner Park
7311 Hwy 100
warnerparks.org
Ten miles of
trails across 2,500
acres of Harpeth
hill country
and woods.

....

MARINA

Percy Priest Lake
3737 Bell Rd
percypriestlake.org
Only fifteen
minutes from
downtown, boat
rentals available at
Nashville Shores.

....

LIBRARY

Downtown Branch
615 Church St
library.nashville.org
Noted architect
Robert Stern chan-
nels Athenian spirit
in grand space.

....

SWIMMING HOLE

Cummins Falls
Cummins Mill Rd
Jackson County
Near Cookeville,
Blackburn Fork

River plunges 50
feet into a
gorgeous pool.

....

STARGAZING

Dyer Observatory
1000 Oman Dr
dyer.vanderbilt.edu
Second Friday
of the month,
telescope nights in
Radnor State Park.

....

COUNTRY DRIVE

Natchez Trace
Hwy 100 w of Nashville
nps.gov/natr
Started with bison
trek, then Indians
and soldiers, now
Sunday drivers.

....

SMALL TOWN

Leiper's Fork
Old Hillsboro Rd
& State Hwy 96,
visitleipersfork.com
Rural village of
antique loots and
country-store song-
writer nights.

....

FARMERS MARKET

Nashville
Farmer's Market

900 Rosa L. Parks Blvd
nashvillefarmersmar-
ket.org
Growers park trucks
362 days a year,
downtown tradition
since 1800's.

....

SMOKEHOUSE

Rice's Country Hams
12217 Lebanon Rd
ricescountryhams.com
Open October
through Christmas,
traditional salt-cured
hams, whole or sliced.

....

SPORTING EVENT

Iroquois
Steeplechase
Percy Warner Park
iroquoisesteeplechase.org
Over 25,000 seersuck-
ered-and-sundressed
tailgaters every May
since 1941.

....

DRIVE-IN

Stardust Drive-In
310 Purple Tiger Dr
stardustdrivein.com
Half-hour drive
from city, starlit
silver screen March
to November.

» EXPERTISE «

BARBER

Parlour & Juke

521 8th Ave S #302

parlourandjuke.com

Antique barber chairs, juke-joint décor, smooth straight-razor shaves.

....

GUITAR FIXER

Joe Glaser

434 E Iris Dr

615-298-1139

Famous roster (Keb Mo, Vince Gill) kept his shop busy post-flood 2010.

....

YOGA

Leah Lillios

1011 Fatherland St

kaliyugayoga.com

Small classes with discounts to grad students and the recently laid off.

TAILOR

Stitch It

4101 Hillsboro Cir

615-292-3008

Jeff Loring and Co. are courteous, timely, adjacent to Green Hills Mall.

....

INTERIORS

Rachel Halvorson

@rachelhalvorson

rachelhalvorson.com

Garden & Gun covergal designed homes for Ronnie Dunn and Dan Auerbach.

....

ARCHITECT

Nick Dryden

2520 White Ave

daad-group.com

Clients include Peter Nappi, Burger Up, as well as major Gulch work.

MECHANIC

Polly's Service Center

3200 Belmont Blvd.

615-297-4901

Owned-operated by native Nashvillians since 1959, where Belmont crosses 440.

....

FASHION DESIGN

Amanda Valentine

@valentimes

amandavalentine.com

Fashion designer-bass player has styled for Levi's and Ben Affleck.

....

DISC JOCKEY

Eddie Stubbs

Mon-Fri 7pm-12am

AM-650

wsmonline.com

Historian-DJ of old-time country gold on the original Opry station.

WOODWORK

Christian Fecht
fechtdesign.com
Hand-hewn hickory
and maple tables,
chairs and bowls, for
folks like Pinewood
Social.

....

POET

Mark Jarman
poets.org/mjarm
Tenured Vanderbilt
professor published
Bone Fires in 2010.

....

GRAPHIC DESIGN

Matt Lehman
@matt_lehman
mattlehmanstudio.com
Design clients
include *Esquire,*
CMT, *Monocle,* and
Maroon 5.

....

TATTOO

Josh Woods, Black 13
209 10th Ave S
black13tattoo.com
Self-taught co-
owner of Cummins
Station shop has a
bold colorful style.

FARMER

Johnny Howell
Nashville Farmers
Market, 615-242-1623
Stringbean-slender
family farmer
trucks in tomatoes
from Bellevue.

....

LETTERPRESS

Bryce McCloud
624 Ewing Ave
isleofprinting.com
One-man shop
puts modern
touch on classic
woodcut-and-
printing trade.

....

PEDIATRICIAN

Elizabeth
Triggs, M.D.
4322 Harding Pike
greenhillspeds.com
Vanderbilt-trained
physician joined
Green Hills Pediat-
rics in 1985.

....

SOUND ENGINEER

Vance Powell
408 E Iris Dr
sputniksound.com

Three Grammy
wins, mixes for
Jack White's
label, sports
epic beard.

....

COUTURE

Manuel Cuevas
800 Broadway
manuelcouture.com
Still-active costume
icon of Johnny Cash,
Elvis, Hendrix, The
Beatles.

....

STYLE BLOG

Pennyweight
elisejoseph.com
@pennyweight
Native Elise
Joseph has lent her
impeccable taste to
lifestyle brands like
Madewell.

....

TREE SURGEON

Ruel Jones
515 Tankersley Ave
qualitytreesurgery.com
Removal and prun-
ing by an honest-to-
God champion tree
climber.

ALMANAC

A deep-dive into the cultural heritage of Nashville, featuring lists, timelines, historical hearsay, scientific data, newspapers, telegrams, and other curious miscellany

SONGBIRDS OF NOTE

Species	Coloration ... Habitat ... Song
Acadian Flycatcher	greenish back...mature woods...shrill "peet-sah"
American Goldfinch	bright yellow...weedy fields...twittering warbles
American Robin	gray with red breast...common yard..."cheerup cheerily-cheerily"
Eastern Bluebird	blue back, orange chest...open woods, parks...series of raspy scolds
Eastern Meadowlark	brown-flecked back, yellow breast...grassy farmland..."Spring of the year"
European Starling	glossy, speckled black...lawns, sidewalks...sings and mimics
Indigo Bunting	male is strikingly blue...edge of cultivated land...warbling series, sharp "spik"
Killdeer	brown, black circles on throat...parking lots, golf courses...piercing "kill-deer"
Mourning Dove	soft brown, black accents...backyards, woods...sad cooing
Nashville Warbler	drab olive back, yellow chest...spring and fall woods... "seewit-ti-ti-ti"
Northern Mockingbird [*state bird*]	gray and white...dense berry shrubs...original and mimicked song
Tufted Titmouse	silver-gray, rust-color flanks...canopy woods... "peter-peter-peter"
Whip-poor-will	grayish-brown with white necklace...open wood...lands quick chirping, sounds like the name
White-eyed Vireo	olive green top, yellow sides...thickets, the margins..."quick with the beer check"

CIVIL WAR

Three years after marrying, Rachel Carter Craighead watched Union troops march into Nashville from her doorstep. Her banker father refused to take an oath of allegiance to the Union Army and was sent to penitentiary, and her brother John died from wounds taken in Perryville. Throughout the war, Rachel kept a journal, which is available for public reading at the Tennessee State Archives.

SUNDAY FEBRUARY 1ST
- 1863 -

Since I last wrote in my journal — we have been left desolate. It is with my face in my hands and my hands bowed to the dust that I have to write the sad, sad, news, that has broken our hearts — my precious Brother is dead! Can it be true? How nobly he died— Oh Lord, that our tears could recall him and our prayers give him life. His noble and high-strung spirit took its flight to the realms of bliss, Sunday [18 January] at 4 o'clock. Nothing less can be said of him than he died gloriously. But what is there to look forward too — what a wilderness will life be these long-long dreary days — to us, and what is there beyond — nothing but desolation. Oh! They have killed my only brother, our dear soldier boy— I feel like I must die too.

THE NATCHEZ TRACE

"ATTACKS ON TRAVELERS"
Tennessee Gazette
May 18, 1803

On Friday last Mr. Reubin White of this county, on his return from Natchez, was killed near Swan river, [about 50 miles from this place] by a party of Indians and a white man. He had a considerable amount of money with him on a pack horse, which, by the exertions of two others who were in company with him, was saved. On Sunday the Mail-carrier and another man were fired on near the same place supposed by the same party, but luckily escaped without injury. This is the third attack on travelers of that road within a few weeks past.

A sunken path pounded flat over centuries by bison, soldier and tramp, the now-protected NATCHEZ TRACE PARKWAY extends 444 bucolic miles, in two lanes, from Natchez, Mississippi (Mile Post 0) to Belle Meade, in Nashville (Mile Post 444). In Tennessee, the miles ribbon out past waterfalls and the log cabin where Meriwether Lewis died. nps.gov/natr

---

HANK WILLIAMS

Only 29 when he died of hemorrhages to the heart,
Hank Williams still casts a ghostly light into modern rock 'n roll.

WESTERN UNION

MRS J K SMITH=
199 SMITH PLACE APT 77
WILLIAMS COURT=

COME AT ONCE HANK IS DEAD=
MOTHER=

"HILLBILLY STAR,
SONG WRITER, DIES
IN AUTO"
Nashville Banner,
January 1, 1953

Hank Williams, hillbilly star and hit tune composer, died in his car near Oak Hill, Va., this morning according to the Associated Press. First reports said Williams suffered a heart attack while riding with a friend, Charles Carr of Montgomery, Ala. Carr, chauffeur for the radio and recording star, said the [29]-year-old Williams became unconscious in his automobile near Oak Hill. He was dead on arrival at an Oak Hill hospital at about 7 p.m. today. The body of Williams will be sent to Montgomery for burial.

Williams had been scheduled to make a personal appearance in Charleston, W. Va., last night. However the plane on which he was traveling returned to Knoxville, Tenn., after bad weather prevented a landing at Charleston. State Trooper G.R. Lilly said Carr related that he and Williams then set out to drive by automobile to Canton.

Williams was star of the "Grand Ole Opry" here for about three years until his contract was terminated in August 1952. Jim Denny, artists service representative for the "Opry," said Williams was dropped for failing to appear on scheduled radio shows and missing personal appearance performances.

The lanky Western star wrote such hit songs as "Cold, Cold Heart," "Manson On The Hill," "Move It On Over," "Jambalaya," and "Lovesick Blues."

He was known in country music circles as "king of the hillbillies."

In 2011, artists including
Jack White and Lucinda
Williams released a tribute
album of unrecorded
material called THE
LOST NOTEBOOKS OF
HANK WILLIAMS.

COMMON SALAMANDERS

Cave............................reddish orange body, irregular dark spots, long tail
Spotted ....rows of yellow-orange spots length of body
Smallmouth ....dark coloration specked with gray, narrow head
Tiger ....prominent yellowish-green blotches, dark brown body
Hellbenders .... nocturnal with large flat head and tiny eyes
Mudpuppies .... brown-black body with large spots, dark eye-gill line
Dusky ....variable color, hind limbs noticeably larger than front
Two-Lined ....dingy yellow color with two strong black lines
Longtail...................light to brownish yellow, herringbone tail patterns
Four-Toed .... gray to orange-brown with dark spots, white underside
Zigzag.............gray-brown with zigzagging reddish pattern along back
Mud .... coral to brown color, clean round black spot
Eastern Newt .... aquatic adults yellowish green, red or black spots

UNITED RECORD PRESSING

One of the last ten American presses in operation, United Record Pressing runs five days a week. Its machines stamp out 40,000 records a day in the grindingly loud factory adjacent to the Nashville Sounds' ballpark.

(1) Recordlike lacquer rotates as music is played

(2) Electric signals from master recording travel through a needle

(3) Needle etches groove into lacquer, replicating sound

(4) Lacquer coated in silver, spun in nickel bath

(5) Metal disc, or mother, is produced with ridges instead of grooves

(6) Mother used to create the ridged stamper

(7) Stamper, a negative of the recording, placed in hydraulic press

(8) Tiny pellets of vinyl melted at 250 degrees into biscuits

(9) Biscuit placed between stampers, squished for two seconds

(10) Music is imprinted and excess biscuit trimmed off

RACCOONS

In the 1950's, Disney turned frontiersman Davy Crockett into a bonafide TV hero. Boys clamored for coonskin hunting caps, and as "Crockettmania" spread to Great Britain, some 5,000 caps sold per day. The price per pound for raccoon fur jumped from 25 cents to $8. Perhaps in response to popular culture, the legislature made the common raccoon, Procyon loter, *that nocturnal furry-masked bandit, the official Tennessee state mammal in 1971.*

HOW TO MAKE A COONSKIN CAP

- Measure distance around the head plus one inch [C]

- Draw the circle on the skin-side of the coon, just under its head.

- Cut out the circle for the top of the cap

- To make the sides, divide C by 2 to identify the proper length of the sides [S]

- In the center of the coonskin, cut out 2 rectangles S inches by 4 inches

- Using a blanket stitch, sew the 4-inch edges of Side 1 and Side 2 together on both ends of the rectangles, skin-side out

- Using a blanket stitch, sew the top of the hat to Side 1 and Side 2 along the S measurement of each side

- Cut the tail off the coonskin and using a blanket stitch, attach the tail to desired area of the hat

- Wear with full confidence

PERSONAL NOTE FROM JOHNNY CASH

Musician Johnny Cash wrote this informal credo in the mid-1990's. Today the note hangs in his daughter Rosanne's New York apartment.

I must remember that my "Internal Prime Time" is early morning and very late at night. This is when I think best, –when I should write.

Sometimes it is <u>very</u> important that I just sit around and do <u>nothing</u>

<u>Rest</u> every midday.

CRIME

"THE EXECUTIONS OF HENRY AND MOSES"
THOUSANDS ASSEMBLED

Nashville Gazette
February 22, 1851

The Execution Yesterday — Between 11 and 12 o'clock yesterday, Henry and Moses [two slaves accused of murder] were taken from the county jail, and conveyed, under strong escort, to the gallows, which had been erected about 1 mile from town, in the vicinity of the Murphreesboro turnpike and Brown's Creek. About four or five thousand persons assembled on the ground, as we are informed by our reporter, among whom we regret to say, were a large number of females. A short time before the execution, the Rev. Mr. Brown, a Catholic priest, ascende the scaffold, and addressed a few words to the assemblage. He stated his firm conviction, as a minister of the gospel, that the prisoners were both innocent of the crimes for which they were about to suffer death.

The reverend gentleman then went through the ceremony of prayer, after which the halters were adjusted upon the necks of the criminals. Henry and Moses then each addressed a few words to the crowd, in which they persisted in declaring themselves innocent. Henry said: "Gentlemen, I am innocent. I never did any murder, and when you take my blood, you take innocent blood." Moses said: "I have but one word to say: I never murdered any man; if I did, I don't know it. That's enough." After these declarations were made, the rope which supported the scaffold was cut by the sheriff, and the criminals were launched into eternity.

We trust this execution will be the last which the people of Nashville will ever witness.

TOMATOES

Forty minutes west of Nashville, Marianna's in
Dickson carries a sampling of heirloom tomato seeds.

Airyleaf	Dolly Parton	Mary Robinson's
Aunt Gertie's Gold	Duggin White	Nebreska Wedding
Amich Paste	Ernie's Plump	Northern Lights
Banana Legs	Ernie's Pointed	Orange Strawberry
Barrao Black	Georgia Streak	Pearl's Yellow Pink
Bandy's Old Yellow	German Bi-Color	Peppermint
Basinga	Golden Cherokee	Perkstine Orange
Beach Boy	Green	Piedmont Pear
Bear Claw	Green Pear	Portuguese Neighbor
Beefsteak	Green Zebra	Prue
Big Rainbow	Grub's Mystery	Rento
Big Zebra	Halfmoon China	Roman Candle
Brad's Black Oxheart	Hawaiian Pineapple	Sarnowski Plum
Brown's Large Red	Indian Moon	Strawberry
Bull Sac	Ivory Egg	Stetson Yellow
Candy Stripe	Jersey Devil	Super Sioux
Cherokee	Kellogg's Breakfast	Stoke's Green
Chico	Kiev	Scarlet Topper
Chuck's Yellow Earl	Liberty bell	Spark's Yellow
of Edgecomb	Little Lucky	Spear's Tennessee De
Cleota Yellow	Ludmilla's Red Plum	Summer Cider
Cream Sausage	Margarita	Tiger Paw
Diener	Marizol Gold	Wagon Wheel

NASHVILLE SOUNDS

LOCAL BAND   WHAT THEY SOUND LIKE

Apache Relay .... East Nashville meets the Avett Brothers
Leagues .... Melodic pop with Beach Boys vocals
Sugar and the Hi Lows .... Modernized Memphis soul duo
Shelly Colvin .... Emmylou sound with SoCal spirit
Wild Cub .... Jubilant synth with a 80's MJ feel
Escondido .... Pop radio with a desert landscape vibe

"3 MORE SEIZED IN SIT-IN EFFORT"
Nine A&I, Fisk Students Fail At Two Places

The Tennessean
- Dec 3, 1962 -

Three students — two from Tennessee A&I and one from Fisk University — were arrested yesterday afternoon when they and six others attempted to stage sit-ins at downtown restaurants.

City police said the students were arrested after they refused to move away from the door of Herschel's Tic-Toc restaurant on Church Street, the scene of a sit-in demonstration Saturday which ended with two arrests.

Yesterday's demonstration, unlike other sit-in attempts of the past week and a half, were well in progress before police arrived on the scene. The demonstration occurred while most city policemen were directing traffic for Nashville's Christmas parade.

Those arrested on a charge of failing to obey officer's orders to move on were:

John Robert Lewis, 22, Fisk student, from Troy, Ala. Lewis is chairman of the Nashville Non-Violent Committee.

Lester Gene McKinnie, 22, of 920 28th Ave. N.

Frederick Leonard, 20, also of 920 28th Ave. N.

All were released after posting a $5 bond each. They are scheduled to appear in City Court at 10 a.m. today.

Five co-eds were in the group which attempted earlier to sit-in at Cross Keys Restaurant on Sixth Ave.

When they moved to the Tic Toc, the students were met at the door by a restaurant employee, Johnny Rebel, who blocked the entrance and said:

"We don't serve Niggers here and you ain't going to get inside."

Two of the group, McKinnie and Leonard, attempted to get inside the restaurant but were driven out when Rebel turned a fire extinguisher on them.

In the second-floor CIVIL RIGHTS ROOM at the Nashville Public Library, visitors can watch six different documentaries, including an hour-long 1960 NBC news program about the Nashville sit-ins. [615 Church St., library. nashville.org, free]

POLITICS

More than 200 reporters covered The State of Tennessee versus John Scopes in July 1925, including H.L. Mencken, who famously dubbed it the "Monkey" trial. The case, the first ever to be broadcast on national radio, focused American attention on tiny Dayton, 150 miles southeast of Nashville. It was one of the hottest summers on record, and proceedings were moved outside under the shade of willow oaks, where Judge John Raulston opened the trial with prayer and a reading of the first 31 verses of Genesis. Creationism and Evolution were clearly on trial. And though later overturned on a technicality, substitute teacher John Scopes was found guilty on July 8, and was fined $100, in accordance with Section 2 of Mr. Butler's law. The ACLU funded his defense.

CHAPTER NO. 27.
HOUSE BILL NO. 185.
[BY MR. BUTLER]

AN ACT prohibiting the teaching of the Evolution Theory in all the Universities, Normals and all other public schools of Tennessee, which are supported in whole or in part by the public school funds of the State, and to provide penalties for the violations thereof.

SECTION 1. Be it enacted by the General Assembly of the State of Tennessee, That it shall be unlawful for any teacher in any of the Universities, Normals and all other public schools of the State which are supported in whole or in part by the public school funds of the State, to teach any theory that denies the story of the Divine Creation of man as taught in the Bible, and the teach instead that man descended from a lower order of animals.

SECTION 2. Be it further enacted, That any teachier found guilty of the violation of this Act, Shall be guilty of a misdemeanor and upon conviction, shall be fined not less than One Hundred $ [100.00] Dollars nor more than Five Hundred [$500.00] Dollars for each offense.

SECTION 3. Be if further enacted, That this Act take effect from and after its passage, the public welfare requiring it.

Passed March 13, 1925.
W. F. Barry, Speaker of the House of Representatives.
L. D. Hill, Speaker of the Senate.

Approved March 21, 1925.
Austin Peay, Governor.

BASEBALL

In his high-flying, mythic prose, Grantland Rice recaps the city's greatest ballgame in the Tennessean. Nashville beat New Orleans, 1-0, for the Southern League crown in front of 12,000 fans at Sulpher Dell.

*"ECHOES OF THE
FLAG FIGHT"*
By Grantland Rice
September 20, 1908

It was a grand victory, nobly fought for and honestly, fairly, squarely and worthily won. While Sitton and McElveen were the bright particular stars of the day, every man on the team was right on the job from gong to gong, playing star ball, eating everything that came toward them, handling difficult chances with ease, and backing up every position that needed it. Groom fought like a noble, squire-like knight, as fearlessly and well...The Volunteers went up and down the circuit, moving like a well regulated and well oiled piece of machinery...not a scintilla of friction anywhere. The "spirit of fight till the last armed foe expires" was instilled in every man's heart. With the best pitching staff in the league to back them up, they knew they were bound to win the pennant.

HEADQUARTERS

Asurion Telecommunications

Baldwin Piano Company

Captain D's

Central Parking Corporation

Cokesbury Publishing

Corrections Corporation
of America

Country Music Television

Cracker Barrel

Dollar General

Firestone Tire and Rubber

Gaylord Entertainment

Gibson Guitars

Griffin Technology

Hobby Lobby International

Hospital Corporation of America

Ingram Industries

Lifeway

Louisiana-Pacific

Nissan North America

Pinnacle Financial

Purity Dairies

SESAC Performance Rights

Sitel Customer Service

Thomas Nelson Publishing

CHRISTMAS MENU

Before it burned in 1961, the Maxwell House Hotel feted guests such as Henry Ford and Theodore Roosevelt. Its famous Christmas dinner remains storied for the bountiful, if not odd, delicacies.

CHRISTMAS, 1879

"A MERRY CHRISTMAS TO ALL."

TABLE D'HOT

Mobile Bay Oysters on the Half Shell.

SOUP Green Sea Turtle. New Orleans Gumbo.

FISH Mackinaw Trout, boiled. Anchovy Sauce.

OYSTERS Raw Oysters. Escaloped Oysters. Oysters in Champagne. Broiled Oysters. Oysters with Fine Herbs. Stewed Oysters.

HOT RELIEVES Turkey, Oyster Sauce. Back Bones and Turnips. Leg of Young Lamb au Petit Pois. Venison Chops with Prunes.

HOT ENTREES Les Filets de Boeuf, Braises, aux Champignons. Prairie Grouse, with Spanish Olives. Legs of Young Rabbits. Hard Shell Crabs, Deviled. Charlotte of Apples, a la Parisienne. Sweet Breads.

COLD SIDE DISHES Les Cervelles de Veau. French Mushrooms, en Aspic. Boston Baked Pork and Beans. Sliced Boned Capon.

GROSSE PIECES FROIDE [Ornamented.] Boned Wild Boar's Head, a la Royale. Lobster Salad, a la Russe. Boned Turkeys. Buffalo Tongues. Pate de Fois Gras, a la Strasbourg.

HOT RELISHES Mayonaise de Volaille, au Celery. Rice Croquette, Orange Flavor. Les Petite Omelets.

ROASTS Adam Coe's Xmas Beef. Suckling Pig. Loin of Veal, Madeira Sauce. Domestic Ducks. Saddle of Kentucky South Down Mutton. Green Goose.

GAME Leg of Cumberland Mountain Black Bear, Sauce Poivrade. Tennessee Opossum,

Old Virginia Style.
Kentucky 'Coon,
Devil's Sauce.
Roasted Quail.
Saddle of Min-
nesota Venison.
Canvas-back and
Red-head Ducks.
Blue-wing and
Wood Ducks.

VEGETABLES
Baked Sweet
Potatoes. French
Green Peas. Stewed
Tomatoes. String
Beans. Yarmouth
Corn. Mashed Irish
Potatoes. French
Asparagus, Butter
Sauce. Oyster Plant.
Succotash.

PASTRY Mince
Pie. New England
Pumpkin Pie. Peach
Tartlets.

PUDDINGS
English Plum
Pudding. Indian
Pudding.

SMALL PASTRY
Lady Cake.
Wafer Jumbles.
Jelly Drops.
Rosalind Cakes.

CONFECTIONS
Peach Candy. Pepper-
mint Drops. Cream
Bonbons. English
Walnut Bonbons.
Candy Mottoes.

*JELLIES
AND CREAMS*
Charlotte Russe.
Russian Jelly.
Maraschino Jelly.
Apple Brandy Jelly.

*FRUITS AND
DESSERT*
Malaga Grapes.
English Walnuts.
Figs. London
Layer Raisins.
Oranges in Sherry
Wine. Green
Gages. Pine Apples
in Champagne.
Vanilla Ice Cream.
Frozen Roman
Punch.

French Coffee.

CANDY MAKERS

1897 Nashville confectioners, William Morrison and John Whar-
ton, engineer a heated bowl to spin out feathery sugar. Originally
called "Fairy Floss," their cotton candy invention debuts at the 1904
World's Fair.

. . . .

1912 First-ever combo candy bar introduced by Howard Campbell
and Porter Moore. Milk chocolate, peanuts, marshmellow, and cara-
mel is swaddled in tin foil and named Goo Goo Clusters.

. . . .

2010 The Bang Candy Company's Sarah Souther whips up first
batch of homemade pink marshmallows with rose water and minty
cardamom seeds. Two years later, she opens confectionary cafe at
Marathon Village.

RYMAN AUDITORIUM

1894	Rev. Sam Jones revival
1901	New York Metropolitan Opera
1907	Teddy Roosevelt lecture
1913	Helen Keller sellout
1918	Charlie Chaplin speaks
1924	Harry Houdini performs
1943	Grand Ole Opry moves in
1945	Earl Scruggs joins Bill Monroe
1946	Chet Atkins debuts
1948	Little Jimmy Dickens' first show
1949	Bob Hope and Doris Day
1949	Hank Williams receives six encores
1954	Elvis receives mild applause
1957	Louis Armstrong performs
1969	The Johnny Cash Show begins
1974	Last official Opry broadcast
1980	Filming of Coal Miner's Daughter
1992	Centennial Anniversary
1994	Completes major renovation
1998	Tammy Wynette memorial service
2003	Coldplay sellout concert
2003	Memorial service for Johnny Cash
2010	Hosts 48 Opry shows after flood
2012	Mumford & Sons three-night residency

CICADAS

When The Great Southern Brood, also known as XIX, emerged in May 2011 from 13 years underground, the red-eyed, molters covered the city like a plague. Nashville couldn't ignore the million-bug chorus or the "Sing. Mate. Die." bumper stickers. They were underfoot. Jammed in AC units. Swarming hospital helicopters. The intensity hit Led Zeppelin levels at night and dogs feasted during the day. But just weeks after the loud, zombielike return, the cicadas disappeared, gone again, save the lonesome stragglers and crispy brown-yellow exoskeletons. That is until 2024, when the next generation will burrow up once more.

BURGERS

Burger Up............................ Benton's bacon, Jack Daniel's maple ketchup
Rotiers .... Six-decade griddle patties on French roll
Fido ....Beef-lamb, caramelized fennel, fig aioli
McCabe's Pub .... Swiss cheese patty melt on sourdough
Brown's Diner .... Griddle-fried in a doublewide trailer
Krystal...Late-night sack of the mini-burgers
The Pharmacy .... Farm egg, ham slice, local bacon

---

SHAWNEE

*Algonquian-speaking Shawnee
settled along the Cumberland in
the late 1600's and early 1700's,
before trade wars with Europe-
ans, Chickasaw, and Cherokee.
The Shawnee left Middle
Tennessee for good in 1745.*

English	Shawnee-Algonquian
Dog	Wii'ši
Bison	Meθoθo
Deer	Pšekθi
Raccoon	Ha'Ðepatii
Bear	Mkwa
Snake	maneto
Turtle	skutelawe
Sun	Kiišθwa
Moon	Tepeki kiišθwa
Water	Nepi
Man	Hileni
Woman	Kweewa
Red	Mškwaawi
Yellow	Hoθaawa
White	Waapa
Black	Mkateewa

LOST & ENDANGERED SPECIES

LOST

....

Woodland Bison
Eastern Elk
Carolina Parakeet
Passenger Pigeon
American Mastodon
Wooly Mammoth
Tennessee Riffleshell
Eastern Puma

ENDANGERED

....

Gray Bat
Coosa Moccasinshell
Flying Squirrel
Red Wolf
Spruce-fir Spider
Red-cockaded
Woodpecker
Green Pitcher Plant
Tennessee Purple Coneflower

TENNESSEE HUNTING CALENDAR

SPECIES	SEASON	LIMITS
Squirrel (fox, red, gray)	Aug. 27-Feb. 29	10 per day
Rabbit	Nov. 5-Feb. 29	5 per day
Deer (bow)	Sep. 24-Jan. 1	3 antlered bucks per year
Deer (gun)	Nov. 19-Jan. 1	3 antlered bucks per year
Elk	Oct 15-Oct. 19	1 per year, permit by lottery*
Bear	Oct. 31-Nov. 3 / Dec. 1- Dec. 14	1 per year
Beaver, Coyote, Striped Skunk	year-round	no limit
Fox, Mink, Muskrat	Nov 18-Feb 29	no limit
Bullfrog	Year-round	20 per person per night
Raccoon, Oppossum	Sep 16-Feb 29	2 per person per night
Canada Goose	Sep. 1-Sep. 15	5 per day
Wood Duck	Sep. 10-Sep. 14	2 per day

*Illegal killing of wild elk subject to 11 months in jail

*The taking, killing or illegal possession of hawks, owls, songbirds, endangered species, or any other species for which a season is not set [e.g. snakes] is prohibited.

*Hunting, trapping, or possession of albino deer is prohibited.

NASHVILLE THE FILM

Robert Altman directed the Oscar-nominated black comedy about country music, big breaks, and American politics. Filming across the city from July to September 1971, the climactic scene gathers the city's fictional music stars for an open-air concert at the Parthenon.

ACTORS	CHARACTERS	RESEMBLANCES
Henry Gibson	Haven Hamilton	Roy Acuff, Hank Snow
Ronee Blakely	Barbara Jean	Loretta Lynn
Timothy Brown	Tommy Brown	Charley Pride
Keith Carradine	Tom Frank	Kris Kristofferson
Karen Black	Connie White	Lynn Anderson

SUFFRAGE

In the dog days of August, 1920, Sixth and Union, site of the Hermitage Hotel, was the nerve center of the women's suffrage movement. Forty-two years of toil hinged on Tennessee's legislature becoming the final ratification vote for the proposed Nineteenth Amendment. On Friday, August 13, President Woodrow Wilson voiced support of the cause via a telegram from his staffer J.P. Tumulty to suffragist Carrie Chapman Cato at the Hotel.

WESTERN UNION TELEGRAM
RECEIVED AT HERMITAGE
HOTEL BRANCH

59NFY AH 56 GOVT

THE WHITE HOUSE
WASHINGTON DC 633 PM
AUG 13 1920

MRS CARRIE CHAPMAN CATT
HERMITAGE HOTEL NASH-
VILLETENN

THE PRESIDENT HAS JUST
WIRED THE FOLLOWING
TO THE SPEAKER OF THE
HOUSE NASHVILLE QUOTE
MAY I NOT IN THE INTEREST
OF NATIONAL HARMONY AND
VIGOR AND OF THE ESTAB-
LISHMENT OF THE LEADER-
SHIP OF AMERICANS IN ALL
LIBERAL POLICIES EXPRESS
THE EARNEST HOPE THAT
THE HOUSE OVER WHICH
YOU PRESIDE WILL CONCUR
IN THE SUFFRAGE AMEND-
MENT

J P TUMULTY
827 PM

THE BEST PART about that culture-clashing vote: Both Suffragists, who pinned yellow roses to their shirts, and their opponents, who wore red ones, hustled for weeks in Nashville, and went into the August 18 vote literally counting the legislative lapels. After two deadlocked roll calls, the youngest member of the House, Harry Burn, finally broke ties with the red roses and cast an historic 'yea.' The Amendment passed, 50 to 49. He hid in the Capitol attic as chaos ensued, and when finally asked about his flip, Burn told reporters it was at the gentle spurring of another telegram, one wired by Febb Burn, his mother.

PRESIDENT NIXON & THE GRAND OLE OPRY

*Less than six months before his resignation, President
Richard Nixon shared the stage with Roy Acuff to
dedicate the brand new Grand Ole Opry House.*

MARCH 16, 1974

ROY ACUFF: I think it would be very appropriate if all of us would sing "Happy Birthday" to Mrs. Nixon, but I won't be imposing if, should I ask you, Mr. President, will you please play the piano for us?

PRESIDENT NIXON: Well, in this very professional company, I am a little embarrassed to try to do that thing there. I haven't even learned to play this thing. It is a Yo-Yo. In the key of G.

[The President plays "Happy Birthday" on the piano. Then, the President takes a Yo-Yo from his pocket and hands it to Mr. Acuff, who was known for doing tricks with a Yo-Yo during his performances.]

THE PRESIDENT: Just so that you will know-as you know, my wife's name is Pat, and her father was Irish, and he called her "St. Patrick's babe in the morning." So she always celebrates her birthday on St. Patrick's

Day. So, I can't play this song at all, but these fellows know it in the key of G, also. That is the only key I know, incidentally.

So, if you will join us in this song, I think you will recognize it when I start it. Just let me get a chord.

[The President plays "My Wild Irish Rose."]

MR. ACUFF: He is a real trouper, as well as one of our finest Presidents. You are a great man. We love you.

MR. ACUFF: [handing the President a Yo-Yo] Now let it come over this way. Hold your hand like this. [Laughter] We are not in any hurry. He don't need to get back up there quick anyway. [Laughter] We need him down here for a while. Now, turn your hand over and let it ride. Now jerk it back.

THE PRESIDENT: I will stay here and try to learn how to use the Yo-Yo. You go up and be President, Roy.

STAGENAMES

Motivations for celebrity noms de guerre include spelling issues, ethnicity, family affiliation, memory, originality, and flash.

STAGE NAMES	REAL NAMES
Big & Rich	William Kenneth Alphin and John Rich
Patsy Cline	Virginia Patterson Hensley
John Denver	John Henry Deutschendorf
Wynonna Judd	Christina Ciminella
Patty Loveless	Patty Lee Ramey
Ira & Charlie Louvin	Ira & Charlie Loudermilk
Randy Travis	Randy Traywick
Shania Twain	Eileen Regina Edwards
Conway Twitty	Harold Jenkins
Kitty Wells	Ellen Muriel Deason
Reese Witherspoon	Laura Jeanne Reese Witherspoon
Tammy Wynette	Virginia Pugh
Young Buck	David Darnell Brown

ANDREW JACKSON'S DUEL

On May 30, 1806, future president Andrew Jackson faced a rival horse breeder in a gentleman's duel. Charles Dickinson was said to be the finest shot in Tennessee. It's also said that the deadly row was prompted by public affronts, spoken by Dickinson, about both Jackson and his wife, Rachel. (The offender called her a "bigamist," alluding to gossip over an imprecise divorce from her first husband.) In the duel, Dickinson shot first, wounding Jackson above the heart. Jackson kept his footing, but his gun misfired. He then shot an arguably iniquitous second time into the man's abdomen. Dickinson would die hours later. For Jackson, historians posit that both the lodged bullet and the two-shot strategy plagued him until he died in 1845. Over 200 years later, local historians dug up what they believe to be Charles Dickinson's final remains in a West Nashville front yard. They found a finger bone in the disturbed earth but neither of the bullets.

HERMITAGE HOTEL OPENS

The grand debut of Nashville's first million-dollar hotel brought national attention to the city, as well as New York's Waldorf-Astoria orchestra, which performed in the lobby.

**NASHVILLE BANNER
SEPTEMBER 16, 1910**

*HERMITAGE
HOTEL OPENING
Small Army of Workers,
Clatter of Hammers and
Tools Sound like Storm*

Without doubt the busiest place in the world barring the Panama Canal is the Hermitage Hotel to-day. The big hostelry will be ready for business to-morrow evening. It will be thrown open to the public at 6 o'clock for dinner and at that time the public will get first peep at the wondrous beauty of the great structure. That Nashville will gasp in surprise cannot be gainsaid.

Every energy is being lent to have it ready, and Manager Timothy Murphy says it will be ready. The tip is given out, in fact, that by to-morrow evening one will hardly recognize it as the same hotel. The clatter and roar of hundreds of hammers and chisels and other tools make the interior of the big hotel sound like a hailstorm. Everywhere there is intensified activity. All is bustle and hurry and stir. From the kitchen in the basement to the top floor things are busy, very busy. Most of the big hotel is already finished, and by to-morrow evening wonders will have been wrought.

In 2003, a $17-million renewal project elevated the Hermitage Hotel to modern grandeur.
**231 SIXTH AVENUE NORTH,
THEHERMITAGEHOTEL.COM,
FROM $220.**

RENOWNED NASHVILLE RESIDENTS

Thomas Edison	Nicole Kidman	James Weldon Johnson
James K. Polk	Jimi Hendrix	W.E.B. Du Bois
Al Gore	Ulysses S. Grant	Wilma Rudolph
Oprah Winfrey	Jesse James	James Dickey
Bettie Page	Ann Patchett	Red Grooms

WAR CORRESPONDENCE

We are two lonely soldiers who have returned from Hawaii a few weeks ago and who are now stationed in the remote section of the United States...sixty miles from the nearest town and, worst of all, we are situated on an island from which we cannot venture to any kind of recreation.

We are now on "limited duty," because of our injuries sustained in the battle of Pearl Harbor.

If you will publish this, I am sure some of your readers would surely care to correspond with a couple of lonely soldiers. We can write about some of our horrible experiences of the battle of Pearl Harbor and how we were injured.

PVT. Ralph A. Bever.
PVT. CARNEY P. SMITH.

Dec. 1942

TO THE MEMBERS OF THE
ELKS LODGE NO. 72:
JAN. 9, 1943 TIME: 10:47 A.M.

Dear kind friends,

I received the generous box of cigarettes, soap, powder, shaving cream and playing cards you sent me. Words cannot express how much I appreciate your kindness. I thank you for this wonderful box. Although, I never had much of a Christmas — I am enjoying Christmas today. I want to thank you from the bottom of my heart.

My folks are dead. I am 21 years of age. Am suffering from a bullet wound in my spine. Am still in the hospital since Pearl Harbor. I wish to forget that incident.

I would like to hear from any of the members of the Elks. I am no Elk, but when I get well I will certainly become a member. Again I thank you ever so much for the swell box.

Your grateful friend, Ralph Bever

Jan. 1943

MAYO'S FRIED PIES

When Mahalia Jackson's Glori-Fried Chicken chain of restaurants shuttered in 1970, E.W. "Elzy" Mayo decided to keep the soul food menu alive in Nashville. To the chicken, Elzy added his mother's turnover-style fried pies, made from scratch daily. Pretty soon, the line out the door wasn't for Mahalia's yardbird; it was Mayo's Fried Pies that were a new Nashville foodway. He folded the knuckle-beaten dough over homemade sweet potato, peach, or apple mash, crimped the edges tight with a fork, and deep-fried them to golden brown. Elzy Mayo died in 2010, two days before Christmas. He was 93 years old. Today, his nephew, a man who goes by "Top Dawg," continues making Mayo's fried pies, crimping fork and all. He sells them for 99 cents out of a bright yellow trailer at 2008 Jefferson Street. Rarely do the pies last through a normal lunch hour.

CORNELIA FORT

Nashvillian Cornelia Fort was an aviator in the exclusive Women's Auxiliary Ferry Squadron during WWII, a program that freed up male pilots for combat. Before her ferrying post, Cornelia was on a mid-air training exercise when the Japanese bombers attacked Pearl Harbor in 1941. She landed the plane without injury.

MAR 17, 1943
LOS ANGELES, CA

THINGS ARE LOOKING UP. I'M GOING AS CO-PILOT ON ONE OF THESE DC 3'S (ARMY C-47) NANCY HAS BEEN GUINEA-PIGGING FOR US & FLEW A P-51 (THE FASTEST PURSUIT WE HAVE). I LOVE EVERYTHING ABOUT THE POST, THE PEOPLE, THE PLANES AND MY GREY CONVERTIBLE!

CORNELIA

Four days after this postcard was mailed, Cornelia Fort's plane collided with a BT-13 over Texas and she was killed. She is the first female pilot in American history to die on active duty.

THE FUGITIVES & THE AGRARIANS

*In the 1920s an informal Nashville literary salon,
made up largely of Vanderbilt professors and scholars,
produced an influential modernist poetry magazine
called* The Fugitive, *and, later, stoked a revisioning
of Southern ideals in a book of contentious essays called*
I'll Take My Stand. *One member, a young Robert
Penn Warren, would go on to win two Pulitzers and
become United States Poet Laureate.*

POET	POEM
Donald Davidson	"Twilight on Union Street"
Stanley Johnson	"A Sonnet of the Yellow Leaf"
Merrill Moore	"Cumae"
John Crowe Ransom	"Bells for John Whiteside's Daughter"
Alec Stevenson	"He Who Loved Beauty"
Allen Tate	"Ode to the Confederate Dead"
Robert Penn Warren	"Bearded Oaks"
Jesse Wills	"The Watchers"

CONTENTS OF A CONFEDERATE
SOLDIER'S KNAPSACK

- ⤇ Gum blanket or poncho
- ⤇ Shelter half and rope
- ⤇ Extra Shirt
- ⤇ Extra Socks
- ⤇ Underdrawers

- ⤇ Sleeping hat
- ⤇ Small gloves
- ⤇ Lotion, shoe polish
- ⤇ Handkerchief
- ⤇ Sewing kit
- ⤇ Pipe and tobacco
- ⤇ Good pocket knife

- ⤇ Plate, fork, spoon
- ⤇ Boiler cup
- ⤇ Toothbrush
- ⤇ Testament
- ⤇ Hemp twine
- ⤇ Canteen
- ⤇ Medications

COUNTRY MUSIC BILLBOARD HITS

Year	Track	Artist
1944	Smoke On The Water	Red Foley
1945	I'm Losing My Mind Over You	Al Dexter
1946	New Spanish Two Step	Bob Willis
1947	Smoke! Smoke! Smoke! [That Cigarette]	Tex Williams
1948	I'll Hold You in My Heart	Eddy Arnold
1949	Lovesick Blues	Hank Williams
1950	I'm Moving on	Hank Snow
1951	Slow Poke	Pee Wee King
1952	The Wild Side of Life	Hank Thompson
1953	Kaw-Liga	Hank Williams
1954	I Don't Hurt Anymore	Hank Snow
1955	In the Jailhouse Now	Webb Pierce
1956	Heartbreak Hotel	Elvis Presley
1957	Gone	Ferlin Husky
1958	City Lights	Ray Price
1959	The Battle of New Orleans	Johnny Horton
1960	Please Help Me, I'm Falling	Hank Locklin
1961	Walk on By	Leroy Van Dyke
1962	Don't Let Me Cross Over	Carl Butler and Pearl
1963	Love's Gonna Live Here	Buck Owens
1964	My Heart Skips a Beat	Buck Owens
1965	What's He Doing in My World	Eddy Arnold
1966	Almost Persuaded	David Houston
1967	All the Time	Jack Green
1968	Folsom Prison Blues	Johnny Cash
1969	My Life [Throw It Away If I Want To]	Bill Anderson
1970	Hello Darlin'	Conway Twitty
1971	Easy Loving	Freddie Hart
1972	My Hang-Up is You	Freddie Hart
1973	You've Never Been This Far Before	Conway Twitty
1974	There Won't Be Anymore	Charlie Rich
1975	Rhinestone Cowboy	Glen Campbell
1976	Sweet Dreams	Emmylou Harris

Year	Track	Artist
1977	Luckenbach, Texas	Waylon Jennings
1978	The Gambler	Kenny Rogers
1979	I Just Fall in Love Again	Anne Murray
1980	He Stopped Loving Her Today	George Jones
1981	9 to 5	Dolly Parton
1982	Always on My Mind	Willie Nelson
1983	Jose Cuervo	Shelly West
1984	If You're Gonna Play in Texas	Alabama
1985	Lost in The Fifties Tonight	Ronnie Milsap
1986	On the Other Hand	Randy Travis
1987	Forever and Ever, Amen	Randy Travis
1988	Eighteen Wheels and a Dozen Roses	Kathy Mattea
1989	A Better Man	Clint Black
1990	Love Without End, Amen	George Strait
1991	Don't Rock the Jukebox	Alan Jackson
1992	Boot Scootin' Boogie	Brooks & Dunn
1993	Chattahoochee	Alan Jackson
1994	Don't Take the Girl	Tim McGraw
1995	Go Rest High on That Mountain	Vince Gill
1996	Blue	LeAnn Rimes
1997	Carrying Your Love with Me	George Strait
1998	Wide Open Spaces	Dixie Chicks
1999	Amazed	Lonestar
2000	I Hope You Dance	Lee Ann Womack
2001	Where Were You	Alan Jackson
2002	The Good Stuff	Kenny Chesney
2003	Three Wooden Crosses	Randy Travis
2004	Live Like You Were Dying	Tim McGraw
2005	Better Life	Keith Urban
2006	Jesus, Take the Wheel	Carrie Underwood
2007	Stay	Sugarland
2008	Our Song	Taylor Swift
2009	Need You Now	Lady Antebellum
2010	The House That Built Me	Miranda Lambert
2011	If I Die Young	The Band Perry
2012	Somethin' Bout a Truck	Kip Moore
2013	Cruise	Florida Georgia Line

MAPS

*Hand-illustrated maps to show where trusted locals
go for live music, comfort food, artisan wares,
the great outdoors, and city history*

FISK JUBILEE SINGERS

Charlotte Ave.

Broadway

WSM

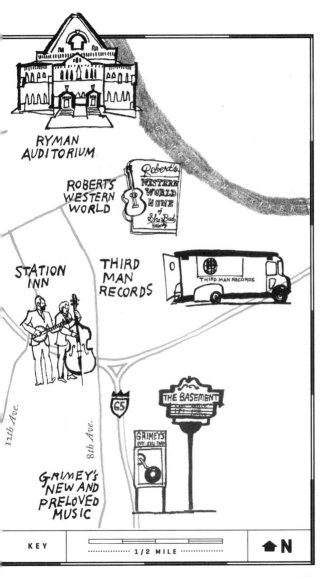

RYMAN
AUDITORIUM

Robert's
WESTERN
WORLD
HOME
of
Shu-Bud
Hillbilly

ROBERTS
WESTERN
WORLD

STATION
INN

THIRD
MAN
RECORDS

THIRD MAN RECORDS

12th Ave.

8th Ave.

65

THE BASEMENT

GRIMEY'S
BUY-SELL-TRADE

GRIMEY'S
NEW AND
PRELOVED
MUSIC

KEY

.... 1/2 MILE ....

⬆ N

⫸ MUSIC ⫷

*Nashville still circles the block for vinyl, packs out a bluegrass joint
(even on a Tuesday), and reveres its hometown gospel choir.*

THIRD MAN RECORDS
Jack White brings a part Slash, part Wonka vibe to Nashville, but his biggest impact is a bee-yellow vinyl shop and don't-box-us-in label (Wanda Jackson, The Greenhornes). *623 7th Ave S, thirdmanrecords.com.*

....

STATION INN

In a town bedrocked with institutions, none has remained its original self quite like this cinderblock bluegrass grotto in the Gulch. Fire-picking mandolin, banjo, and bass, seven nights a week. *402 12th Ave S, stationinn.com*

....

GRIMEY'S NEW AND PRELOVED MUSIC
Holiest of record-store holie's, Grimey's goes 100k deep in vinyl, staffs Nick Hornby characters, and rocks a basement venue. *1604 8th Ave S, grimeys.com*

....

ROBERT'S WESTERN ROOM
Yes, it's touristy. But Robert's and the other Broadway honky-tonk brethren deserve the traffic. Robert's owner fronts the house band, Brazilbilly, and packs 'em in. *416 Broadway, robertswesternworld.com*

....

RYMAN AUDITORIUM
Built in 1892 by a born-again riverboat captain, the Ryman's past includes 31 years of Opry shows (and Houdini!) in the wooden-pew hall that Garrison Keiller called "God's own listening room." *116 5th Ave N, ryman.com*

....

FISK JUBILEE SINGERS
Since 1871, the a capella choir has sung Negro spirituals all over the world, drawing from HBCU undergrads at Fisk, a cultural fount in North Nashville. *fiskjubileesingers.org*

....

WSM 650
There's no better radio slot than Eddie Stubbs' nightly show on this circa-1925 station. Stubbs speckles his old-time AM playlists with front-porch bits of Opry lore. *WSM 650 AM, wsmonline.com*

LOCAL EXPERTS *Leagues frontman Thad Cockrell, and singer-songwriters Jessie Baylin and Courtney Jaye, are part of a tightknit bond of Nashville musicians pushing past the city's country sound.*

⟫ FOOD ⟪

Nashville's most beloved restaurants, new and old, stick to simple, soulful fare, with the menu stretching from red-hot fried chicken to belly ham pizza.

CITY HOUSE
This Germantown spot shows off best during the chef's laidback Sunday suppers, when the house-cured meats are center stage. *1222 4th Ave N, cityhousenashville.com*

PRINCE'S HOT CHICKEN SHACK
Nashville began this yardbird foodway, and, if one spot owns the best origin story, it's here: their recipe was cooked up by a stilted lover. *123 Ewing Dr, 615-226-9442*

ROTIER'S
Cornered between the Parthenon and Vandy's frat row, Rotier's is a cozy, dimlit burger monument, still serving huge griddle-hot patties on French bread with glass bottle Cokes. *2413 Elliston Pl*

MARCHÉ
Chef Margot McCormick [Café Margot] puts her contemporary spin on southern brunch in the sunniest and most aromatic room in town. P.S. Ordering the red velvet cake at breakfast is encouraged. *1000 Main St, marcheartisanfoods.com*

MAS TACOS POR FAVOR
Teresa Mason's DIY Winnebago delivers gourmet street food, and her Eastside taqueria has quickly become beloved by her neighborhood. *732 McFerrin Ave, eatmastacos.com*

ARNOLD'S COUNTRY KITCHEN
If you don't know the term "meat-and-three," get thee to Arnold's. South's most wonderful use of math, as taught by country cookin'. Mac and cheese lovers: Bring your bibles. *605 8th Ave S, 615-256-4455*

NASHVILLE FARMER'S MARKET
Truckloads of homegrown melons, pattypan squash, peppers and pumpkins hauled in seven days a week just north of downtown. *900 Rosa Parks Blvd, nashvillefarmersmarket.org*

LOCAL EXPERT *Chef Tandy Wilson, a four-time James Beard Foundation Best Chef Southeast nominee and charcuterie disciple, opened City House in 2008.*

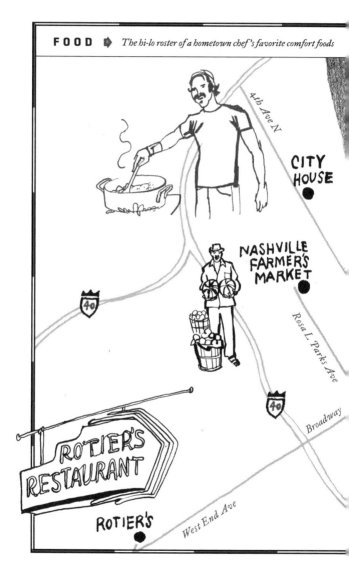

4th Ave N

CITY
HOUSE

NASHVILLE
FARMER'S
MARKET

Rosa L Parks Ave

40

40

Broadway

ROTIER'S
RESTAURANT

ROTIER'S

West End Ave

Dickerson Pike

PRINCE'S HOT CHICKEN SHACK (3 miles)

MAS TACOS POR FAVOR

McFerrin Ave.

MARCHE ARTISAN FOODS

24

Woodland St.

8th Ave S

ARNOLD'S

ARNOLD'S COUNTRY KITCHEN

KEY

3/4 MILE

N

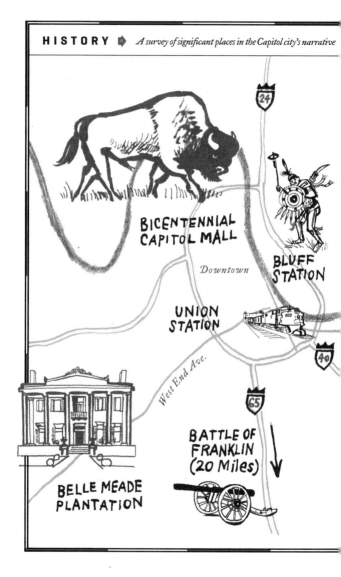

THE HERMITAGE

Lebanon Pike

KEY

······· 2 MILES ·······

▲N

⚡ CLASSIC CUISINE ⚡

Where to find the Creole and Cajun signatures,
from beignets to turtle soup to crispy fried chicken.

GUMBO
LIUZZA'S BY THE TRACK
A very dark roux layered with cooked-to-order seafood, locally-made sausage, okra and thirteen seasonings whose combination was concocted by owner Billy Gruber, who passed away in 2016. *1518 N Lopez*

....

SEAFOOD PO BOY
PARKWAY BAKERY
This century-old joint on the bayou has mastered the art of the fried shrimp po-boy. Eat it "dressed" with Zapp's chips and a cold bottle of Barq's. *538 Hagen St*

....

BEIGNETS
CAFÉ BEIGNET
Fried golden pockets lighter and chewier than their legendary kin at Café du Monde. Plus the line is way shorter. *334 Royal St*

....

TURTLE SOUP
COMMANDER'S PALACE
This dark, rich, soul-filling soup is made with real turtle meat,

spinach and hard-boiled eggs. A drizzle of sherry is recommended. *1403 Washington Ave*

....

FRIED CHICKEN
WILLIE MAE'S
Fried to order, the chicken at this legendary 5th Ward lunch joint is served with shatteringly crunchy crust overlaying still-juicy meat. *2401 St Ann St*

....

MUFFULETTA
CENTRAL GROCERY
The old Sicilian grocery is the home of this local sandwich, layered with ham, salami, cheese and marinated olive salad on a Leidenheimer bun. *923 Decatur St*

....

RED BEANS & RICE
DOOKY CHASE
Historically, Monday was when women put the ham bone left over from Sunday to simmer in a pot of kidney beans. Go to Dooky Chase's for the matriarch Leah's flavorful take. *2301 Orleans Ave*

LOCAL EXPERT *Author Sara Roahen takes readers on a deliciously researched tour-de-fork in her 2008 book of essays,* Gumbo Tales, *published by W.W. Norton.*

WELL HELLO THERE, NEW ORLEANS

....

In our recent Nashville print
run, we found a mysterious snafu
on page 56. The good news? You
now know the 7 classic restaurants
we love most in NOLA. For
Nashville history intel, flip
this insert over. Sorry for our
mistake and safe travels!

—*Taylor Bruce,* WILDSAM

⪢ HISTORY ⪡

A complex lineage includes tribes along the Cumberland, Confederate soldiers in battle, and President Andrew Jackson's plantation.

BICENTENNIAL MALL

The prehistoric Sulphur Lick [adjacent to the State Capitol building] attracted the buffalo, elk, and deer, which in turn attracted native American hunters. Topiary bison mark the spot today. *600 James Robertson Parkway*

....

BATTLE OF BLUFF STATION

The Bluff Station [colloquially called Fort Nashborough] was a log stockade built by the white settlers, who, in 1781, narrowly fought off a harrowing Chicamauga attack. Replica downtown is a bit folksy. *170 1st Ave N*

....

THE HERMITAGE

Andrew Jackson's home and grounds exemplifies the shift from primitive life to antebellum gentility in the South, and his Greek-Revival mansion is the fourth-most visited Presidential landmark in America. *4580 Rachel's Ln, thehermitage.com*

BELLE MEADE PLANTATION

Monumental jewel in Nashville's toniest neighborhood, the limestone mansion with a rose-colored roof was the stately residence of a notable thoroughbred breeder on the "Queen of Tennessee plantations." *5025 Harding Pike, bellemeadeplantation.com*

....

UNION STATION

Built in 1900, the soaring rail terminal served eight tracks, until the Victorian-Romanesque structure was renovated as an historic hotel. Also, once sported two alligator ponds in the lobby. *1001 Broadway, unionstationhotel-nashville.com*

....

WSM BARN DANCE

Started in 1925 by National Liberty Insurance ["We Shield Millions"], the AM650 station broadcast the Saturday-night Grand Ole Opry, effectively the launch of Nashville as Music City. *wsmonline.com*

LOCAL EXPERT *Paul Clements spent 10 years researching and writing The Chronicles of the Cumberland Settlers, a 300-year retrospective on Nashville history. It was published in 2012.*

⫸ MAKERS ⫷

*From handsome neckties, killer chocolate, and raw denim with family roots,
Nashville's small-batch vibe encourages a craftsman entrepreneurship.*

IMOGENE + WILLIE BLUE JEANS
Kentucky-born couple Matt and
Carrie Eddmenson have been
touted wide, from GQ to Rolling
Stone, and their Americana-flecked
collections grow larger [and more
impressive] every season. *2601 12th
Ave S, imogeneandwillie.com*

EMIL ERWIN LEATHER BAGS
Emil quit a desk job in 2008 to
wrestle cowhides into satchels,
briefcases, and totes, that now sell
at Barney's. He moved his studio
to Marathon Village in 2012. *904
Buchanan St, emilerwin.com*

OTIS JAMES NECKTIES
These wool and linen patterns
bring to mind Faulkner and
Fitzgerald, who'd both appreciate
the hand-sewn story of this Marathon tie shop. Stop in, Otis'll
teach you the perfect knot. *1006
Buchanan St, otisjamesnashville.com*

OLIVE AND SINCLAIR CHOCOLATE
Chocolatier Scott Witherow

stone-grinds cacao, cuts in
spices [Ceylon cinnamon, sea
salt, espresso beans] and wraps
with beautiful Ye-Olde-Wonka
paper. *oliveandsinclair.com*

PETER NAPPI BOOTS Nappi's kudu
leather boots, crafted in Tuscany
with a rigorous commitment to
Italian cobbling detail, are sold in
a former Germantown abbatoir.
1308 Adams St, peternappi.com

YAZOO BREWERY BEER Owner Linus
Hall studied hops in Brooklyn
before opening his microbrewery,
and now his Gulch taproom pulls
from 18 taps, the best a citrusy
Hefeweizen. *910 Division St,
yazoobrew.com*

HATCH SHOW PRINT POSTERS
This Broadway concert poster
shop is an unofficial country music
shrine. Looking at the gigantic
presses and inky hickory blocks, it's
impossible to not wax nostalgic. *224
5th Ave S, hatchshowprint.com*

LOCAL EXPERTS *Designers Matt and Carrie Eddmenson
raised seed money to launch Imogene + Willie by sewing
and selling 250 pairs of custom-fit jeans in 2009.*

PETER
NAPPI

Monroe

3rd Ave. N.

EMIL
ERWIN
+
OTIS
JAMES

11th Ave. N.

Hatch
PATSY
CLINE

HATCH
SHOW
PRINT

Broadway

40

YAZOO
BREWERY

12th Ave. S.

YAZOO

IMOGENE
+WILLIE

OLIVE
AND
SINCLAIR

McGavook Pike

Gallatin Ave.

KEY

1 MILE

N

DOWN
TOWN
NASHVILLE

CLIMB
NASHVILLE ●

Harding Road

440

2 Ave. S.

65

WARNER
PARKS

RADNOR
LAKE

65

DUCK RIVER
(47 miles)

SHELBY
BOTTOMS

Shelby
Ave.

CANEY FORK RIVER
(52 miles)

40

440

Bell Road

HAMILTON
CREEK

KEY

4 MILES

N

✠ ADVENTURE ✠

Locals escape the city in all directions, by floating canoes, casting fly lines, and exploring the rugged corners of the Highland Rim.

WARNER PARKS

Hilly acres near Belle Meade host the Iroquois Steeplechase every May, as well as a summer of bluegrass. But year round, this is a runner's heaven. *7311 Hwy 100, friendsofwarnerparks.com*

....

SHELBY BOTTOMS

Multi-use stretch along the river includes golf, sports fields, free bike rentals, greenway access, and a rad green-roofed nature center. For Eastsiders, this is Central Park. *1900 Davidson St, nashville.gov/parks*

....

DUCK RIVER

Laidback paddling 45 minutes south of Nashville on one of the most biologically diverse rivers in North America. A Saturday float in the hot of July is unforgettable — especially after a day of rain. *4361 Hwy 431, riverratcanoe.com*

....

CANEY FORK RIVER

Below Center Hill Dam, the beautiful tributary is stocked with tailwater rainbows and browns from March to December. Plan for an hour drive on I-40. *800-238-2264, flysouth.net for reports*

....

CLIMB NASHVILLE

Basecamp indoor spot in Sylvan Park with 50 top-rope routes, 50-75 boulder problems, 50 lead climbs, all changed out regularly. Post-climb beers at McCabe's Pub. *3600 Charlotte, climbnashville.com*

....

HAMILTON CREEK BIKING

Two single-track courses cut through limestone outcroppings, cedar groves, all with airport flyovers. Percy Priest Lake is nearby for cliff-jumping. *webelevation.com/hamcreek*

....

RADNOR LAKE

Built for steam locomotives in 1914, then kept as a sportsman's club, Radnor Lake is now a 1,200-acre sanctuary of trails south of town. *1160 Otter Creek Rd, radnorlake.org*

LOCAL EXPERTS *The best gear shop in town is Cumberland Transit, where Allen, Lori, Becki, Jason, and Co. give sound advice for local adventures. 2807 West End Ave, cumberlandtransit.com*

⫸ ARTS ⫷

Nashville's visual arts repertoire is noteworthy, from O'Keefe's endowed collection at Fisk to the Cheekwood Museum and Sculpture Trail.

FISK'S STIEGLITZ COLLECTION

Georgia O'Keeffe donated 101 pieces [worth over $70 million today] to Fisk University in 1949, the bequest which included works by Picasso and Cezanne. In 2012, half ownership of the collection was sold. 1000 *17th Ave N*, 615-329-8720

....

RYMER GALLERY

The best of the downtown galleries includes the playful work of crayon sculptor Herb Williams, who cuts and creates with the sticks upstairs. Lively gallery crawls held every first Saturday of the month bring in big crowds. 233 *5th Ave N*, *therymergallery.com*

....

FRIST CENTER

The Art Deco post office was redesigned as a city architectural signature. The non-collecting museum hosts new exhibitions every eight weeks. Under 18 admitted for free. *919 Broadway, fristcenter.org*

SMALLEST ART GALLERY

Started in 2008, the solar power street display is barely bigger than a suitcase, but brings for-real artists to Hillsboro. Most people walk right by and never notice this gem. 1807 1/2 *21st Ave S*, *smallestartgallery.com*

....

TOMATO FEST

East Nash shindig, founded by Art & Invention gallery owners nearby, attracts over 18,000 visitors every August, all in homage to the state fruit and its creative juices. *Woodland Ave/Five Pts*, *tomatoartfest.com*

....

CHEEKWOOD SCULPTURE TRAIL

Fifty-five acre garden, funded by Maxwell House coffee family, holds largest collection of William Edmondson statues in the world. Perhaps the most valuable shade in Davidson County. 1200 *Forrest Park Dr*, *cheekwood.org*

LOCAL EXPERTS *Photographer Caroline Allison and painter Emily Leonard, who show at the Zeitgeist and Rymer galleries respectively, are two of the city's finest emerging artists.*

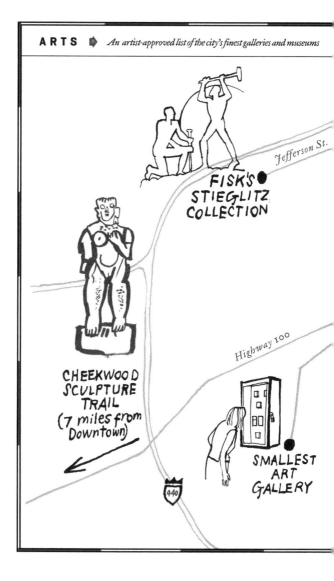

FISK'S
STIEGLITZ
COLLECTION

Jefferson St.

Highway 100

CHEEKWOOD
SCULPTURE
TRAIL
(7 miles from
Downtown)

SMALLEST
ART
GALLERY

440

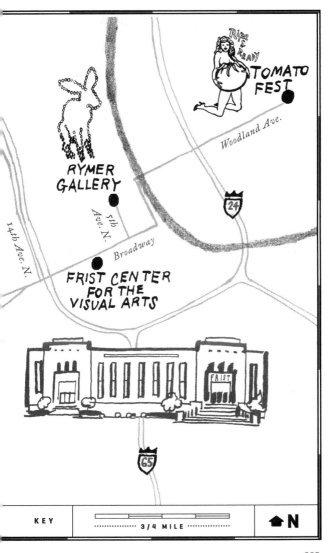

RIPE & READY
TOMATO FEST

Woodland Ave.

RYMER GALLERY

5th Ave. N.

14th Ave. N.

Broadway

24

FRIST CENTER FOR THE VISUAL ARTS

FRIST

65

KEY   3/4 MILE   ◆ N

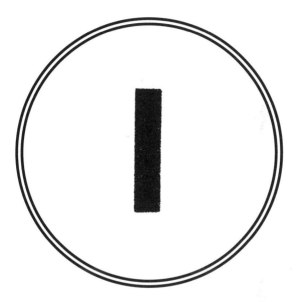

INTERVIEWS

Twelve remarkable conversations about rebuilding Nashville neighborhoods, fishing for trout, growing up Cash, immigrating from Africa, running for Senate, and more

⫸ JIM SHERRADEN ⫷

LETTERPRESS PRINTER

 The Hatch Show Print manager on Waylon Jennings, the seedy days of Broadway, and luck of geography.

TWO BROTHERS came down from Wisconsin with their family, got the place up and running in 1879. Charles and Herbert Hatch.

I SHOWED up 100 years later.

MOVED HERE in 1977 after I gave my poems to Waylon Jennings' guitarist. They said to come on down to Tennessee, and I left the phone hanging in the air. I was the hottest kid back home because I worked for Waylon.

HE EMBODIED the word charismatic. Take your four biggest stars and throw that in Waylon's back pocket and that's what he was. Comfortable with his talent. Most people cannot walk through that forest.

I WAS INTRODUCED to Hatch Show Print in 1984 because I was back waiting tables at Fason's. College degree and all. I needed the shop as bad as the shop needed me.

HATCH WAS dim, bare-bulb, slow. All this history was relatively unrifled through.

WHEN I STARTED it was a typical downtown, like Times Square in the '80s, adult stores, peep shows, seedy. You didn't even want to drink a beer out of a can. We printed posters for Franz Kitty Cats, their XXX movies. *Hannah Does Her Three Sisters*. I'll never forget that one.

YOU CAN'T underestimate the value of the Ryman Auditorium.

OUR MACHINES, our rock maple blocks, the process, it's all the same.

EVERYTHING'S HEAVY in here. Next life, I'm gonna work in a Styrofoam factory.

CHARLES and Herbert, they would recognize the shop, absolutely. They'd get to work.

WHY NASHVILLE? For one, it's within a day's drive of over 75% of the entire U.S. population. That's why all the bands, whether Bessie Smith or the Beastie Boys, play Nashville. It's the damndest thing.

≫ CHRIS NISCHAN ≪

OUTDOORSMAN / GUIDE

A lifelong fly fisherman and naturalist talks about his favorite flock of turkeys, the Caney Fork River, and tying flies.

NOBODY WANTS to hear about the good days, they want to hear the nightmares.

A LADY HOOKED ME in the tongue once, and she was horrified. I cut the leader and gave her a napkin and said, "You're gonna have to hold my tongue so I can get the fly out." When we met back up with her husband, he said, "Honey don't worry about it. That son of a bitch never shuts his mouth."

YOU GOTTA CATCH TWO. One could be a fluke, two is a pattern.

SCUDS, various midge patterns, wolleybuggers, tiny little pheasant tail emergers. I can guide all week out of a Sucrets box.

WHEN I WAS IN high school, we made leghole traps to run on Richland Creek and the South Harpeth. .

MINK ARE really curious.

THERE'S A FLOCK of turkeys over in Percy Warner Park I like to keep tabs on.

IN TWENTY MINUTES any direction, you can be in your own secret spot. Nashville is surrounded by wild places.

ONE SPOT IS ON the Caney Fork River. It's a big ripple in the shape of a keyhole. Beautiful rocks at the head, a big old stump along one side. When the trout are rising, you can stand and watch them. The way the sunlight comes through the trees. Unless you see it, it doesn't make sense. I can't describe it.

EVERY RIVER has its own time.

⇌ TERESA MASON ⇋

TACO TRUCK OWNER

A taco artisan dishes about the keys to cranking a food truck, her first menu, and her secret to hiring employees.

I FOUND THE TRUCK a month after moving back from New York. Turned off the highway at Shelby and saw a 1974 Winnebago was sitting there for sale.

A BAND was using it as a tour van. There was shag underneath shag.

I TRAVELED A LOT after college but always avoided Mexico. It seemed so close to home, didn't feel exotic. But when I finally went, I loved it. The food, the light, the colors. Since then, I've never been anywhere else. I go every year.

A CHICKEN TACO, a quinoa taco, a watermelon agua fresca, and Mexican coke. That was the whole menu.

THE WINNE TOPS out at 35 MPH, so we always take back-roads.

BY NO MEANS have I done Mas Tacos myself. Mom quit her job to help. And I've swindled folks into chopping onions.

IN THE SUMMER all the produce comes from nearby. Sometimes it's as close as the guys down the street bringing us tomatoes.

I'M INSPIRED by simple places. The men that sell churros with just an open flame. You just don't need a lot.

WE'VE BEEN WRITTEN up in Bon Appetit and Rolling Stone. The Black Keys have talked about us. Everybody has taken some ownership in Mas Tacos, which is what makes me most proud.

WHEN WE RAN OUT of fish one day, we just fried up extra avocados for tacos. That's us.

⇒ ALICIA HENRY ⇐

ARTIST | PROFESSOR

The Fisk University art professor on her inspirations, the story of her Victorian home, and race as a theme.

I CAME TO NASHVILLE because of Fisk. I live close enough to ride my bicycle.

I LIVE IN a 1926 house. Supposedly it was built by a white man for his mistress. I like that.

NORTH NASHVILLE is in a transitional time. It's been changing, economically, for a long time. Before integration, this was the area of black lawyers and black doctors. That changed.

THERE'S DEFINITELY not a Starbucks in our neighborhood.

AS A BLACK WOMAN you will for sure see more people of color in my work, but I am most interested in the human condition, and that doesn't stop with race.

PEOPLE ARE WHAT intrigue me.

INSPIRATION is not just about North Nashville. It's the Gulch, it's Germantown, Inglewood, and Green Hills, and East Nashville, it's Bordeaux, West Nashville, Richland, Sylvan Park. I am always sketching things down as I move through the city.

ARTISTICALLY what you always look for is change. That's the heart of it.

IN MY NEIGHBORHOOD, people talk about the old places, the theaters, bowling alleys. I never saw those places.

SPRING TIME at Fisk is lovely. The grass is newly green, the flowering trees are in bloom, the wonderful magnolia trees dot campus.

I TAUGHT ART in Ghana in a village, and everyone knew everybody. It was tiny and isolated. You were very aware of yourself and others.

»» CHELSEA CROWELL «««

SONGWRITER

Johnny Cash's granddaughter on stage fright, the 70's, and the only song she ever wrote with her grandpa.

THE WHOLE TIME I was in utero, I spent in the studio with mom. Her fourth record, Somewhere in the Stars.

I WAS SIX OR SEVEN when I started seeing Nashville's strange celebrity side.

I AM THE ONLY ONE of my sisters who plays music.

EMMYLOU and the Hot Band, Townes Van Zandt, my dad. That era of music is terribly interesting to me. They were tapping into something that had been swept under the rug.

GRANDAD'S APPEAL was the flawed man thing, how he was unafraid to show it to others. He resisted shame. He taught you to not fear flaws. I think it's pretty obvious that it's not because he was Fred Astaire.

MOM HAS SOME of my grandfather's guitars that she's keeping for me. Right now I can't afford to keep them insured.

I GET THE worst stage fright playing in Nashville. To earn any credit amongst your peers, you have to really do your homework. You need to have listened to the Sex Pistols.

I LOVE IRELAND. Same music sensibilities as Nashville without the blasé, been-there-done-that attitude. Even in loud pubs, the Irish pay attention.

I USED TO BE really afraid to fly. To combat the fear, I listened to his music on the airplanes. Something about listening to my grandfather's voice made me feel better.

WE WROTE A SONG together once, a funny song, for my grandmother. We were in Jamaica. My grandma June would always say something like "We're just gonna press on, just gonna keep pressing on," and we wrote a song called "I ain't pressing on, Grandmama," or something to that effect.

....

SHE WAS VERY, very, very funny. Very lively, very quick. She could turn around a sentence really fast.

....

FOUR MONTHS, I think it was. June passed away in May. Him, in September.

....

HE HAD THIS GIANT picture of her on his bedside table in the hospital. My grandfather was miserable. It would have been more miserable to have him lonely and alone without her for a long period of time.

....

THEY WERE married for almost 30 years.

....

WHEN HE WAS sick he got me really interested in the Civil War. I read all of the letters between Sherman and Grant. He gave me some old soldier photographs. I'd come over and read to him in the ICU.

....

BY THE TIME he got to grandfather age, that's what he wanted to be.

WILL PEDIGO
FILMMAKER

ANYTIME PEOPLE start talking about immigration, it's always the capital I, the us and them thing.

....

THE LARGEST Kurdish population in North America lives in Nashville.

....

THE STRUGGLE TO rebuild is common to everybody, but what each immigrant specifically has for success or struggle is always unique.

....

THE COMMUNITIES are in the southeast corridor along Nolensville Road and Murfreesboro Pike. You'll have a Leocian market next to a Kurdish place. It's just a hodgepodge.

....

RESETTLEMENT is barebones. Basically they have 120 days to get it going, to be self-sustaining.

....

WE STARTED THE Bhutanese film, there were three cars for the entire community of 600 people. By the time we finished, there were 20 cars.

....

PEOPLE ARE experts in survival.

⫸ FARHAN AND MEDINA HUSSEIN ⫷

ENTREPRENEURS | IMMIGRANTS

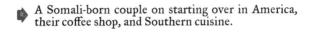 A Somali-born couple on starting over in America, their coffee shop, and Southern cuisine.

FARHAN: We don't have a Somali word for snow. So we say ice is coming from the sky.

MEDINA: When I got to the United States, it surprised me to see black people. I didn't know black people lived in America.

F: The Somali jobs are not good right now. Everybody is driving a taxi. It can be dangerous and bring risks.

M: In Somalia, only women do the household chores. But here it's not. We share. Farhan prefers the cleaning.

M: I appreciate in America when you go to the store and buy something, the salesman say thank you, they appreciate you. I never heard that before.

M: Many younger Somalis, they say, "You don't have a house, or a nice car, you don't have anything. You need the money." They say, "I'm not Somalian, I don't even know where Somalia is. I was born here."

M: A mama told me that she found out that when her little girl left for school she changed. She put the hijab in her backpack.

F: The Somali Coffee Shop is our place. Our people watch soccer and drink coffee and talk. Very much like home.

M: We eat goat meat a lot. Rice with sauce. The spaghetti. I cook everyday. Some American women don't cook. They microwave.

M: When we came to Nashville, we saw that you can have different cultures, that everybody needs to be respected for their own thing.

F: But we don't eat barbeque.

THE SOMALI COFFEE SHOP

....

Nashville Public Television profiled the Somali Coffee Shop in its "Next Door Neighbors" documentary series about city immigrant life. Watch the film at nptv.org, and visit the Hussein's shop at 1040 Murfreesboro Pike for lattes and authentic Somali sambusa.

EMIL CONGDON

DESIGNER / CRAFTSMAN

The leather artisan on starting a business, the smell of saddle shops, and years spent at the Station Inn.

CRAFTING with leather, it's almost like a language that I was just born knowing.

YOU HAVE TO KNOW how it works, how to put pieces together, exactly when to pull, when to push, where to tug.

THAT'S THE ERWIN. My Grandmother was an Erwin. And it's also the name of my hometown. So Emil Erwin, the company, is my name and my place.

THERE WAS a saddle shop in Erwin, and I used to go down there on the weekends. I can still feel it. Walking in the shop and touching the belts and reins and that smell.

FOR MY 20TH birthday I got a sewing machine, a plastic Kenmore that cost $100.

MY FIRST SHOP was a 267 square foot detached garage with exposed insulation and fluorescent lights. And the thing is, as awful as it seemed to me then, it was my dream.

A SIDE of leather is one half of a cow.

I TRY TO CRAFT it where you can't destroy it. Our classic messenger bag takes 12 hours of work. We design them to last several lifetimes.

THE GUY THAT OWNS Horween Tannery in Chicago carries my bag. That's a high compliment for me.

BARNEY'S IN NEW YORK is a long way from Erwin, Tennessee.

MY DAD PLAYED BLUEGRASS, and I grew up hanging at the Station Inn. You don't forget sitting with Bill Monroe.

⋙ NICK DRYDEN ⋘

ARCHITECT | SALVAGER

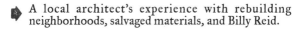 A local architect's experience with rebuilding neighborhoods, salvaged materials, and Billy Reid.

I'M THIRD-GENERATION Tennessee architect. My grandfather studied under Frank Lloyd Wright.

....

WHEN I WAS 11 years old, I collected scrap wood from job sites, chopped it up, and sold it as kindling. The company was called Nick's Sticks.

....

I AM A SALVAGER.

....

LAST WEEK, we bought a barn that somebody was selling on Craigslist, milled it down, and used it on Dan Auerbach's new bungalow.

....

THE GULCH is a low-lying area, near train tracks. Before the condos, the Gulch had become pretty derelict.

....

THE STATION INN was the last holdout.

....

IT'S THE OUTER-LYING stretches that interest me. They're kind of a lost space, industrial brownfields. That is where nobody's looking.

....

I STRIVE FOR place-making. I don't know if it's a real word, but I say it a lot.

....

I'VE GOT THE GRAND POOBAH of salvage stories. We were working with Billy Reid on his New York store, and he needed front doors. I called my friend Garland in Alabama, and he tells me about these three-inch thick, hand-carved doors. Then Garland calls me back, freaking out. 'You're not going to believe this,' he says. 'About three years ago we salvaged a New York building, on Bond. Gutted the place and brought home these doors.' And then he says, 'You aren't going to believe me, but these doors came out of Billy's building, same screw holes.' I immediately called my dad.

≫ BILL FRIST ≪

U.S. SENATOR / PHYSICIAN

The surgeon-statesman on growing up in Nashville, the Civil Rights movement, and fatherly advice.

I WAS THE YOUNGEST of five. By the time I came along, mother and dad had seen everything.

WHEN DAD WAS TEN, his father was killed in a train accident. My grandfather, Jacob Frist. He was the station master, and he was hit helping a woman and her son off some busy tracks. It's not something my father spoke of much.

OUR HOUSE had a certain magic to it. It was my mother's doing.

WE HAD AN OLD blue-and-white station wagon, and, when it snowed, Mother hooked a thick rope to a sled, put the tailgate down, and pulled us for hours through Centennial Park.

I REMEMBER seeing the Civil Rights sit-in's on our television, and Mother saying, "We're gonna be part of the boycott." And we got in the car one day and just drove downtown to Woolworth's. Just to witness it. I was eight years old.

PEOPLE WOULD SPIT on them. They'd burn cigarettes on their heads. When America saw the protesters' poise on television, when I saw that — it had a huge impact on me.

WHEN I WAS SIXTEEN, I was in a bad motorcycle wreck. I hit a car going about thirty miles per hour, headfirst. Broke my wrist, my nose, my right kneecap, and spent about 9 days in the hospital.

I LEARNED about fragility.

FROM THE TIME you take a human heart out to the time you have it beating in a new person, you have four hours. It must be perfect.

YOU CUT THE HEART OUT, you get in an ambulance, you go to the airport, and the engines are running. You get in the airplane, fly two hours, and there's an ambulance ready. In the operating room at Vanderbilt, my partner would do the last cut on the bad heart and I would sew the new heart in. You'd have forty-five minutes, and if it didn't beat within four hours, the patient would die. You've had this heart in an Igloo bucket, just a regular Igloo with ice, nothing fancier. You've been flying through the night. Your adrenaline is going and the chest is wide open. And the recipient's blood, you have to make it go through the new heart to turn the machine off. And this heart, it needs blood. Every second, thousands of cells are dying. So you fill this heart up with blood and then you say a prayer. Very quietly, you just pray that this thing will go. And it starts to shiver a little bit and it starts to quiver a little bit, but you still don't know, and then, all of a sudden, bang! The thing will start beating. It's kind of a miracle.

....

BEING A DOCTOR isn't all that different than being Senator. You interact with all walks of life. You diagnose problems, make a plan, you fix. It's something somewhat absent in Washington today.

WHEN I GOT to Washington, I talked to President Bush and I said if we do nothing about HIV/ AIDS, another 35 million people will die in the next ten years. So in three paragraphs of legislation, we had the single longest commitment by a government to a single disease in the history of the world. And with that, the course of history just changed.

....

I REMEMBER Dad's black doctor's bag. The tools that he needed, the medicines, the thermometer, the stethoscope. And I remember going on rounds with him at night in his black Desoto. Dad walking into houses, the lights going on, him sitting at eye level to the patient. He always sat at eye level and held their hand.

....

IF YOU HAVE BOYS, you've got to be able to say, It's OK to fail.

≫ ANITA SMITH ≪

ADVOCATE

A brave mother's thoughts on fighting chronic homelessness, the power of memory, and how she survived.

I'VE BEEN HOMELESS many times, so many times. I didn't want to die that way.

IT STARTED AT 15 when I got pregnant. I was probably the second girl in the school. I kept the pregnancy hidden for seven months. When he found out, my stepfather wanted me to abort it.

I REMEMBER going to one clinic, to a doctor from Jamaica like my stepfather. He thought the doctor would be cool and consent with it, but he said, "The girl is 8 months pregnant. Are you trying to kill her?"

MY DAUGHTER'S name is Shawna.

MY STEPFATHER shut my mother down. She had been a singer but he told her, "Now you play for me." He shut her whole life down. I was a young and I saw all of that.

A MOTHER'S LOVE is deep. It doesn't matter if she is unfit or whatever. There is still maternal love.

IT MADE ME RUNAWAY. All of it. Runaway, runaway, runaway.

AND I WOULD TAKE that road. One violent relationship after another after another. It's just a vicious crazy cycle. We'd get drunk, all kind of demons.

THE FIRST TIME a man put a knife on me, it didn't even phase me. I remember waking up with slices, and just drinking some more.

I WAS WALKING around dying.

I WALKED INTO a mental health co-op downtown, I finally started talking. I was screaming, Help Me.

I PRAYED THAT God would bless my hands, give me a talent. I know that God is merciful. And

I truly believe that our life is not ours to take. Everything belongs to God.

....

NOW I WRITE my stories for *The Contributor.* One was called "Pain in the Cubicle Next to You." It's so deep. I wrote it in about six minutes.

....

I'M A SURVIVOR.

....

THERE IS A PAUSE we take in life. Sometimes the pause is a long time, but when you release that pause button, life continues. You don't have to die.

....

GOD KEEPS his promises. I may not keep mine, but he keeps his.

The Contributor

....

The Contributor, the highest-circulating street paper in the U.S., publishes two issues a month. thecontributor.org

BOB SNEED
CORPS OF ENGINEERS

....

SUNDAY, MAY 2, 2009, was the single wettest day in Nashville history. Saturday, May 1, was the third wettest day in history. Back-to-back days.

....

TWELVE HOURS of rain, twelve hour break, and another twelve hours of rain. One in a thousand years. Statistically you'll never see it again.

....

BY NOON on Saturday, we couldn't hold the lake level, so we first opened a spillway gate. There were 19 increases to protect Old Hickory Dam. zthe flood was historic.

....

IT'S EITHER coming over your gates or under your gates, and you want to be able to control it.

....

YOU KNEW every time you released more, where it was going, and the damage.

ESSAYS

Four of the city's finest writers, including Tony Earley's ode to East Nashville, Rosanne Cash on an unshakable night, J. Wes Yoder's fear of snakes, and Libby Callaway on couture fashion

»» ALL THOSE DAUGHTERS ««

Written by **TONY EARLEY** | **I LIVE WITH MY WIFE** and daughters in East Nashville, across the Cumberland River from downtown, a mile and a half or so from LP Field, the stadium where the Titans play football. On Sunday afternoons I sit in our kitchen and listen to the games on the radio. The Titans fire a cannon in the end zone whenever they score a touchdown. I hear the boom on the radio, then I jerk open the back door and run onto the deck and hear the boom again, almost inaudible in the distance. It seems to me a small gift, this repetition of joy.

For a while in the mid-1870s Jesse James lived at 606 Boscobel Street, near where I live now. I have yet to talk to anyone in the neighborhood who finds this as interesting as I do.

My older daughter and I ride bicycles to her elementary school, half a mile away from our house. She rides on the sidewalk, I ride on the street beside her. We have flashing white strobes on the handlebars of our bicycles and blinking red lights on the seats. We use the lights on even the sunniest days. She is in the second grade and wears a braid that reaches below her waist and switches side to side when she stands up and walks the pedals. We turn right at the Holly Street fire station—neo-classical, one hundred years old, a landmark—the last firehouse in Nashville where the firefighters slid down a pole when the alarm went off. When I wave at the crossing guard I feel like a cast member on a 1950s television comedy, one of those black and white shows set in a place where nothing bad ever happens.

The Cumberland is a big river, a navigable river, a river where tugboats thread black mountain ranges of coal beneath the bridges. This makes Nashville a river town, I suppose, although I don't believe most of the people who live here think of it that way. Pittsburgh. St. Louis. New Orleans. Memphis. Those are river towns. Nashville, at least to me, feels more like a town with a river. Except during the flood in 2010. We parked at LP Field and walked out onto the bridges and watched it climb, climb, climb into downtown, turning First Avenue heedlessly, tragically Venetian; it bucked with brown, capping waves; it bullied tons of debris toward Kentucky—logs, and accidental barges of unidentifiable trash, and spinning pieces of broken houses, and bright herds of plastic coolers. We wondered, What is the river doing? But now sometimes when I drive home from work on the Gateway Bridge or the Woodland Street Bridge, I don't even remember to look at it.

During the Civil War, Union forces captured Nashville fairly early in the conflict, in 1862. They occupied the city and from Fort Negley gazed suspiciously up and down the Cumberland. The Confederates didn't try to come back until 1865, but in the meantime the town filled up with prostitutes. The Union authorities rounded up the women, put them on the steamboat *Idahoe* and sent them off down the river.

When Jesse James lived in my neighborhood, 606 Boscobel still lay in the town of Edgefield. Nashville smoked and clanged and steamed across the river but had not yet begun eating the small towns around it. Jesse James told people he was a grain speculator named J.D. Howard. His wife Zerelda went by Josie. His neighbors thought he kept awfully nice horses for a grain speculator. His children were named Jesse and Mary. If Jesse James gave aliases to his children, no one remembers what they were.

My older daughter and I want to make it through her five years of elementary school without once taking the car. Twice we have ridden our bikes when it was thirteen degrees, and twice we have ridden when it was ninety-seven. On rainy mornings we walk. We had a close call during an electrical storm last March. While we were putting on our raincoats in the front hallway, I heard my wife say in the kitchen, "Do you really think this is safe?" I looked at my daughter and said, "Run!" By the time my wife made it to the front of the house, we were already across the street and jogging toward school, the air humid and crackling around us, the thunder exploding directly over our heads.

From my back deck I can see the pointy ears of the Batman building eavesdropping above the neighborhood trees; I can see the flickering antennae of fireworks when the Sounds win a baseball game at Greer Stadium, or a concert ends at Riverfront Park. I hear the boom of the fireworks several seconds after the flash; the distant, prolonged cannonade of the finales. Freight trains shout out before crossing Porter Road, then clamber onto the long, high trestle spanning the river at Shelby Bottoms. When the wind is right I can hear the band playing onboard the General Jackson as it paddles boozy tourists back and forth on the river between downtown and Opry Mills. Usually "Rolling on the River." On Saturday nights I can hear the stock cars chasing each other around the track at the Fairgrounds, and always the distant, shushing surf of the Interstate. The police helicopter often thwops overhead, and some nights it draws a bright beam of light across my yard like a brief message from God: I am watching you. Everything will be all right.

When we talk about the flood we say that it was a "five hundred year flood" or a "thousand year flood," but really, how do we know? Every time it rains more than a couple of inches at a time, I start to think about it.

We adopted our older daughter in 2005, in Changsha, Hunan, China, when she was fourteen months old. She had lived until then in an orphanage. A social worker handed her to us and she was suddenly our daughter and we took her back to our hotel and stared at her. When we sat her on the floor she fell over and cried. We had taken classes in Nashville, but nobody had said anything about babies who fell over and cried when you sat them on the floor. We shook plastic keys at her and stacked cups for her and said, Look at that! See how tall! Then we knocked the cups over and stacked them again. We took turns asking each other, Is something wrong with her? We took turns telling each other, She's fine. Don't say that. The next morning she stared at us while we fed her, her brow furrowed. She pooped and we changed her diaper. All right, we said to each other, We can do this. We can do this. We can do this. Now she is eight years old. We ride our bicycles back and forth to her elementary school. I wave at the crossing guard. We wear full Arctic gear on the coldest days, and when we pull on our black fleece helmet liners and neoprene face masks she says, Dad, we look like ninjas.

Bridges connecting East Nashville to downtown, south to north: Gateway, Shelby Avenue, Woodland Street, James Robertson Parkway, and

[*Lower Broadway*]

Jefferson Street. The first evening of the flood we walked out onto the Shelby Avenue Bridge, where my wife spotted a bass boat, empty, still on its trailer, heading in a straight line downstream as if on an urgent errand. The second evening of the flood, the approaches to the Shelby Avenue Bridge were under water. Our older daughter played happily with a friend in the shallow edge of the flood. We backed slowly away from the river as it rose. Our younger daughter still lived in China.

It's the odd week when I don't hear someone mention Hank Williams, and most weeks, at least once, I think the words, The midnight train is whining low. The freight trains crossing Porter Road sound to me more angry and impatient than lonesome, but every time I hear one I listen to see if I have grown sadder. I live in a blue house with a bright green door, with a wife and two daughters who love me. The trains I hear sound mostly like trains. It's been a long time since I felt so lonesome I could cry.

We adopted our younger daughter in 2010, in Nanning, Guangxi, China, three months after the flood. She was three years old, almost four, and had lived until then with foster grandparents, who doted on her. The social workers who came for her told her they were taking her to the park. Then they gave her to us. She was not happy. She wanted to go home. When we stared at her she turned and faced the wall. In Mandarin we said, Are you hungry? Do you need to pee? Do you need to poop? I am your Mommy. I am your Daddy. She is your big sister. We love you. Those were the only things we knew how to say. She shook her head. We took her to the park. We took her sightseeing on a bus with the other American parents in our group and their new, unhappy children. Simon, the Chinese tour guide from the adoption agency, stood at the front of the bus and lectured us on why Taiwan should be part of the People's Republic of China. He thought we could not tell that he was condescending. He thought we could not tell that he thought we were all stupid. Our new daughter would not let me touch her. Our older daughter wished that everyone in China would stop staring at her. I stared at China outside the window of the bus and thought of things I would like to say to Simon before I shoved him. In Nashville, Simon, if that is in fact your real name, I am a professor at Vanderbilt University, a school better than any school in your entire country. In Nashville, Simon, I am the author of four books, one of them published in Taiwan. In Nashville, Simon, I own house with a yard and a flower garden and a building out back for me to write in and I can drink water straight from the tap and not worry about whether or not I am going to die. I reached out to pat my new daughter on the leg. She kicked my hand away. I thought, I am the worst father in the whole world. I am a xenophobe. I am an ugly American. I am forty-nine years old and my children are so young. Simon told us how much money he made. In Nashville, Simon. In Nashville. In Nashville.

In 1952, Hank Williams shot at his estranged wife Audrey with a handgun and almost killed June Carter.

IT'S THE ODD WEEK WHEN I DON'T HEAR SOMEONE MENTION HANK WILLIAMS, AND MOST WEEKS, AT LEAST ONCE, I THINK THE WORDS, THE MIDNIGHT TRAIN IS WHINING LOW.

When I first heard about Jesse James living in the neighborhood, I followed Boscobel Street toward the river. The street, though, peters out near the projects beside a small Bible college. There is no 606 anymore; the house Jesse James lived in burned down during the Great East Nashville Fire of 1916.

My guess is that when my younger daughter starts kindergarten in the fall she will not be interested in riding her bicycle to school when it's cold. Around the time she came here I lost her in the Adventure Science Center. She didn't know how to speak English, and she didn't know my name. When I found her she was standing by herself, seriously examining one of the exhibits. She seemed neither concerned nor particularly glad to see me. When I found my wife, who was also looking for our younger daughter, I asked, Do you think I'm a good father? She looked at our younger daughter, then at me. She said, Sometimes. My wife says that we will not make two trips to the same school to drop off two girls. I'm not so sure. We'll see. We'll cross that bridge when we come to it.

Hank Williams was born in Alabama, moved to Nashville and became a star at the Grand Ole Opry, got himself fired from the Grand Ole Opry, died in the back seat of a car somewhere in West Virginia, and was buried back in Alabama. Yet people who work at the Ryman Auditorium say they have seen his ghost on stage. I would love to spend the night in the Ryman, just to see.

The mockingbird that lives in the hackberry tree in our neighbor's yard does uncanny impersonations of cell phones and car alarms. The mockingbird that lives in the oak tree across from the Holly Street fire station imitates the crossing guard's whistle. "That bird," the crossing guard said one morning, "is going to get somebody killed." The car alarm bird often goes off at three, four o'clock in the morning. You cannot shut it down.

I OFTEN IMAGINE JESSE JAMES RIDING ONE OF HIS FINE HORSES ACROSS THE CUMBERLAND ON WHAT WOULD BECOME THE WOODLAND STREET BRIDGE.

The *Idahoe* wasn't allowed to dock in Louisville or Cincinnati. Nobody would let the prostitutes disembark. Eventually the steamboat returned to Nashville. I used to think it was a funny story—a boatload of hookers with nowhere to go, an exasperated captain, exhausted but happy deckhands, a 1980s Burt Reynolds movie waiting to happen—but I don't think so anymore. All those daughters.

What's left of Fort Negley squats in the woods on top of a hill south of downtown, between the Adventure Science Center on one side and Greer Stadium on the other. During the Civil War it became the biggest inland fort ever built in the United States—18,000 cubic feet of earth, 62,500 cubic feet of limestone. It was constructed by almost 3,000 black men and women: local slaves, and slaves who had fled to safety behind the Union lines, and free black men who were forced at gunpoint to work on the fort. Still, when the fireworks from Greer Stadium flicker and boom above the hill on which the ghost of the fort squats, it is too easy to think patriotic thoughts, rockets' red glare, shock and awe, the just war to free the slaves.

Jesse James sometimes disappeared from Boscobel Street for weeks at a time. When he was home, he ferociously gambled at faro parlors across the river in downtown. He rode one of his two fine horses over the predecessor of the Woodland Street Bridge.

When the tornado chewed through East Nashville in 1998, my wife crouched in our bedroom closet with the dogs we had then. (I stood stupidly on top of two stacked coffee tables and watched through a high window beneath a three-story tower at Vanderbilt because I couldn't stand to not watch.) She said she heard a loud whoosh and that was it. The storm had passed within two hundred yards of our house. On both sides of us trees had fallen on our neighbors' houses, but we didn't lose a shingle. When I made it home from school we walked through the neighborhood with the dogs. Roofs were gone and houses were gone and cars lay smashed beneath fallen trees and live power lines dangled and spat. The power was out in our neighborhood for a week. Nights my wife and I sat in front of the open door of our gas oven, playing cards by candlelight, the dogs curled at our feet, while chainsaws rasped all around us.

Our blue house was built in 1906. Whoever lived here in 1916 must have stood in the front yard and stared at the black smoke to the west, nine, ten blocks away. The wind that day gusted up to fifty miles per hour; the relative humidity was fourteen percent. The people who lived here would have been able to smell the smoke; they would have watched the cinders borne by on the dry, gusting wind. The street they lived on, the street I live on with my wife and daughters, led straight into the heart of the fire.

I have learned, according to the most recent fashionable, politically correct nomenclature that the four of us make up a "conspicuous family." I don't like the phrase. I don't care that my daughters do not look like my wife or me. They are our daughters. I don't feel particularly conspicuous.

Nobody knows for sure exactly how many people Jesse James killed. His children Jesse and Mary were in the house in St. Joseph's, Missouri when the coward Robert Ford shot him in the head. They hid in the kitchen while their mother screamed. Jesse James, Jr. grew up to practice law in Los Angeles; Mary eventually lived out her days on a farm across the road from the farm where Jesse James grew up.

My wife and I have agreed to disagree about the importance of teaching our girls Mandarin. She says it is part of their heritage. I say that any culture that abandons its daughters doesn't deserve them. She says she prays for our girls' biological mothers. I hate that on the other side of the world four people may still think of my daughters as their daughters. My wife says that I shouldn't say such things out loud.

The fire in 1916 burned down 500 houses and left 2,500 people without homes.

Perhaps I am interested in the outlaw Jesse James because of simple proximity, because the 600 block of Boscobel is so close to my house. I often imagine him riding one of his fine horses across the Cumberland on what would become the Woodland Street Bridge. Some of the buildings he would have seen below the bridge to his left still stand on First Avenue.

My daughters each have four names: two given English names (one family name and one first name of a famous woman writer), my surname, and the Chinese names they bore when they were first handed to us. My older daughter's Mandarin name means "peaceful river;" my younger daughter's given Chinese name means "to know writing or literature." Most days I feel that I am participating in a miracle. In China, girls leave the social welfare system in their early teens. It's painfully easy to imagine the bad things that might have happened to my daughters had they been turned out on the street. Bad things could, of course, happen to my girls here, but not if I can help it. I listen for small noises in my sleep, and I am often already awake, listening, when the mockingbird sounds the alarm. We have blinking white strobes on the handlebars of our bicycles and flashing red lights on the seats. We use the lights on even the sunniest days. The National Weather Service sends alerts to my cellphone when the weather turns bad. I worry that our place of safety is not that safe. My older daughter always rides on the sidewalk. The crossing guard stands in the middle of the intersection and holds the traffic while we cross. In the oak tree across from the Holly Street fire station, the mockingbird answers her whistle. These are fine days. These are fine days. These are fine days.

The last time I asked my younger daughter if she remembered any Chinese words she said, No, it's very Spanish, the Chinese.

Several years ago I put the ghost of Jesse James into a short story. He guards the hellhole into which young girls sometimes vanish. I sometimes imagine him riding one of his fine horses across the Woodland Street Bridge into downtown Nashville, his eyes bluer than any eyes should ever be. The buildings on First Avenue look familiar to him but everything else has changed. The Batman building is unimaginably tall. I do not know where he goes once he crosses the bridge.

I usually drive back from Vanderbilt on Demonbreuen Street, or take the Interstate if the traffic isn't bad. Some days, though, I head east on Broadway. On lower Broad I roll down the windows so I can hear the thump and twang of the music spilling from the honky-tonks, the picking and wailing of the buskers on the street corners, the slightly too loud, backslapping laughter of young men who've had too much to drink. The sidewalks are flooded with tourists in cowboy hats and around them neon flashes and hums; bored, diapered horses pull them in open carriages up and down the street; the smell of beer and t-shirts and cheap boots wafts at them out of the doorways; homeless men sidle up and ask for gas money so they can make it back to Clarksville. (Why it's always Clarksville, I don't know. They never ask for money to, say, make it to Murfreesboro or Smyrna.) I stop at the intersection where Broadway dead ends at First Avenue. Ahead of me lies the Cumberland, and across the Cumberland squats LP Field, the stadium where the Titans play football. Some Sunday I'll clock the amount of time between hearing the boom of the cannon on the radio, and hearing it on my deck. My daughters and I will do the arithmetic and figure out exactly how far history has traveled to reach us. If I turn left, First Avenue will take me to the Woodland Street Bridge; if I turn right it will carry me to the Gateway Bridge. If I think about Jesse James I'll turn left; if I'm in a hurry I'll go right. It doesn't matter, really, which way I go from here. Once I cross the river I'm almost home.

TONY EARLEY is the Samuel Milton Fleming Chair in English at Vanderbilt University. He lives in East Nashville with his wife and daughters. His newest story collection, *Mr. Tall*, releases in 2014.

»» THE MOST HUMAN SOUND ««

Written by **ROSANNE CASH** | **I EAT NO MORE THAN** four oranges a
year. They're either too tart or too bland.
Definitely too watery. But in the winter of 1981-1982, in the months of
December and January, I ate nearly a dozen oranges a day. I was heav-
ily pregnant with my second child and I lived in a big log house in the
woods of Middle Tennessee with my then-husband Rodney, my two-
year-old daughter, and my six-year-old stepdaughter. It was one of the
coldest winters on record in the South. The house stayed warm until it
got down to about fifteen degrees; below that, the beautiful old virgin
pine just could not hold the heat. For days on end, as the temperature
hovered around zero, and below, we all stayed close to the stone fireplace in the great room. Rodney kept the fire going (a full-time job)
and the little girls played quietly with their dolls on a green turn-of-
the-century Chinese rug that had been rescued from an old brothel in
Western Kentucky. I sat in a rocking chair next to them, profile to the
fire, a little melancholy, with a bag of oranges on my lap. I ate my way
through a new bag each day, tossing the peels in the flames as I rocked.
The bitter, wild aroma of singed oranges cut into the comber iciness
of the room and soothed me. It was my personal statement against the
chill. I spent many long days like this.

In the first few days of January, three weeks before my due date, my
old friend Randy Scruggs called to ask Rodney and me to participate
in a project he was doing with his dad, Earl, and Tom T. Hall. They
were making a record called *The Storyteller and the Banjoman*. He
invited us to come to his studio and sing a couple of songs. It was
around Earl's birthday and there would be a lot of people there. I was
past the point of maternal glow, way past being cooed at and patted,
and lately inspired only expressions of shock and nervous retreat at
this penultimate phase of gestation. But Randy was my dear friend,
the record would be finished before I delivered my baby, and I

really wanted to sing on it, so I decided to go. I didn't have a coat big enough to close around my belly, and that night turned out to be the coldest one yet of the relentless winter. The air was blue when we stepped outside. The thermometer in the carport registered eleven below zero, and sharp little ice crystals rose in gusts from the hard-packed snow in the driveway. I sulked as we started the long drive to the studio. Rodney,

SHE WAS PALE AND FAIR, AND THOUGH HER DEMEANOR WAS RESERVED, EVEN STIFF, HER EYES WERE DARTING ABOUT AND SHE SPOKE QUICKLY.

experienced with the consequences of unintentionally provoking a woman near the end of her third trimester, gave me a lot of room. It was a very quiet trip.

But it was a wonderful evening. We sang on three songs: "Shackles and Chains," "Roll in My Sweet Baby's Arms," and "Song of the South." Instead of being a sideshow freak, I was treated as a ripe little goddess, and it brought out the best in me. The company of friends and the balm of playing music was liberating, and I was fatigued, but content, when we left. The silence on our return had a decidedly different texture.

We drove, as if in a dream—past the empty country roads at the borders of wide fields enclosed by Civil War-era stone fences, past big, dark, and looming old estates and grand columned mansions that lonesomely adjoined lazy suburban tracts.

We had not seen another car for several miles when we made the turn onto the pike that began the final leg to our hidden house in its miniature valley surrounded by the thick oaks and maples. Rodney drove very carefully as this road was used less than others, and it was still swathed in ice. I was drowsily contemplating having a few oranges by the fire before bed. Suddenly, flashing red lights appeared on the shoulder of the opposite side of the road about a hundred feet ahead. We slowed to a crawl and as we came upon the scene, we saw an ambulance, a car behind it, and, between the two, a man stretched out on his back on the frozen ground. The

[*The Station Inn*]

few people standing over him seemed in no hurry to get him into the ambulance.

"Oh, my God," we both said quietly when we realized the man was dead. Rodney glanced at me. I turned away, profoundly conscious of the baby inside me, reacting to a fierce, primal impulse to protect it from unexpected surges of my adrenaline—the heady, dangerous mix of the hormones of hysteria and fear.

There was clearly no way we could help, so we drove on. A mile or so farther, we were astonished to see, striding toward us up the road, a sturdy-looking middle-aged woman with a tall walking stick. Her gait was so determined, and the stick planted so authoritatively with each step, I could practically hear the drumbeat behind her march. More astonishing still, she was dressed only in a skirt and a sweater: no coat, scarf, or gloves, and she was bare-legged. On her feet were awful brown oxford-type discount-store shoes, shaped carelessly from thin, cheap leather. Only sandals would have been more inappropriate in this weather.

Rodney stopped and rolled down his window. "Ma'am? Can we give you a ride somewhere?"

In a tight, high-pitched voice she said, "Are you sure you don't mind?" and then got into the back seat. She was pale and fair, and though her demeanor was reserved, even stiff, her eyes were darting about and she spoke quickly. "Oh, thank you so much! I'm just going back up the road a little bit. My neighbor there called and said someone had been hit by a car, and my husband was out takin' a walk and now I'm a little worried about him."

I didn't dare look at Rodney, but I could feel that we had both stopped breathing. My heart began to pound, and a queasy feeling rose in my abdomen. Rodney drove the car forward to a little cross street where he could turn around. Fortunately, we didn't have to say anything because the woman was chattering nervously.

"I told him it was too cold to go out walking, but he's stubborn. Said he had to have his evening constitutional no matter how cold it was. Now, are y'all sure you don't mind takin' me back up there?"

"No, ma'am, not at all," I said. "We saw some kind of disturbance back there, but I'm not sure what it was."

"Oh my Lord," she trilled, pleading and panicked. "Now, I don't want y'all to get hurt, too!"

I was struck by that sentence as if by a two-by-four. It still reverberates now, thirty years later: the pitch of her voice, her self-effacing Southern politeness, the tears building behind the contained panic, the uncontrolled sense that danger newly pervaded the entire world. My heart broke for her. In about thirty seconds her entire life was going to detonate and two strangers were sharing her last moments of peace. But it was not my place to tell her.

It was several years later that a friend gave me a tape of Irish keening, which is the sound of women wailing at the graves of their loved ones—long, sustained, unbearable plaintive cries elevated by the deepest sorrow to an art form; the most human sound of the genesis of music. It sent chills down my back and brought tears to my eyes when I first heard it, and the first thing I thought of was her.

She got out of the car that night and a woman came up to her and put an arm around her shoulder and began to talk softly to her. We waited for a moment, then drove away slowly.

Through the closed car windows I could hear her screams: long, deep, circular cries, rising from the roots of her body, like a train whistle disappearing into an endless series of tunnels, like the wrenching Gaelic echoes that hang in the graveyard, like the hiss that escapes from the permanently shattered heart.

I had to borrow from my future that night in protection of my unborn baby. I drew from an unknown reserve of circumspection. "I will feel this later," I thought. And I was unyielding, my hands over my ears, my head bent to my chest.

And I paid, with interest.

On January 25th of that year, I gave birth, after only six hours of labor, to a gorgeous, nearly nine-pound baby girl with enormous bright blue eyes. She was healthy and strong, and I felt proud that I had done my job so well. We named her Chelsea Jane, and I swaddled her warmly and took her home to the big log house. The girls welcomed their little sister and the temperature gradually eased back up into the thirties, where it belonged. My natural indifference to oranges returned abruptly, and the last few left in the bag shriveled and gathered mold before I finally threw them away. I kept the newspaper clipping: " Man Killed By Car On Icy Road," for a week or so longer, and then, that too, I threw away.

Grammy-winning singer-songwriter **ROSANNE CASH** is the author of *Composed*, a memoir. Her nonfiction has appeared in *The New York Times* and *Rolling Stone*. A slightly altered version of this essay was published by The *Oxford American*.

⫸ THE FITTING ⫷

Written by **LIBBY CALLAWAY** | **I WAS 19 WHEN I MET** Jeanne Dudley Smith for the first time. It was the spring of my freshman year in college, just a few months before the start of my debutante season.

My mother and I made the two and a half hour car trip from our home in East Tennessee to Nashville to meet with Jeanne, a designer of some acclaim who sold her line of party dresses at Bergdorf Goodman and Neiman Marcus. I doubt I knew this at the time. Nor did I realize (or care) that she'd made couture frocks for the likes of the late Princess Grace of Monaco.

Looking back now, I realize I didn't know much of anything at 19.

Luckily, Jeanne was used to dealing with clueless girls like me. As a designer, she had a reputation as a "dress whisperer"—someone gifted at helping young women articulate their fashion dreams and desires, and then using the data to design fabulous, one-of-a-kind gowns. Whatever dress archetype her fledgling couture clients had swimming around their heads—be it a frothy fairy queen or a Marilyn Monroe vamp—Jeanne could make it a reality.

I'm tall: I've been 5'10" since eighth grade. But even as a college freshman, I was still learning to feel comfortable in my own skin. Because of this, I was hesitant to meet Jeanne. At the same time, I was curious about the design process. I knew I had the perfect white dress hiding in my imagination, hitching a ride with us in the station wagon as mom and I made our way up I-24 to Nashville. I was anxious to find out what it looked like through Jeanne's eyes.

In the 1970s, my mom was a creative fashion force to be reckoned with. She wore round tortoiseshell glasses and liked to perm her hair. She favored chic smock dresses with dramatic high collars and structured jackets made from old quilts. She had drawers of cool belts and scarves and great vintage jewelry to tie her looks together.

Mom's style was innate. It didn't revolve around labels as much as it did her imagination—and her sewing machine. To wit: when we were little, she'd create thematic holiday looks for herself and my two sisters using reworked one-of-a-kind pieces of vintage clothing and antique fabric she picked up at flea markets. One memorable Easter, we rolled through the front door of our church dressed in an homage to the '30s. Each of us girls was clad in antique straw hats and tea-stained dresses with handkerchief hems that she sewed for us using old linen table clothes, tea towels, and actual vintage handkerchiefs.

Despite being brought up in a home where having unique personal style was encouraged, I never imagined having a career in fashion like I know a lot of girls do. I was not one of those teenagers who grew up stealing her mom's *Vogue*. My mom didn't get *Vogue*. She didn't wear high-fashion designers.

So, when I met Jeanne for the first time, the interaction was revelatory.

On the day of our appointment, Jeanne met us at her front door of her home in Nashville's Belle Meade neighborhood and led us down to her atelier, located on the bottom floor. It was a feminine space appointed with regal French furniture, bookshelves stacked with design reference books and dotted with framed photos of debs, brides and May queens, past and present, and expensive-looking knick-knacks, including two small bronze statues wearing dramatic flapper dresses that our hostess explained were original work by the 1920s designer Erte.

The three of us sat down in front of Jeanne's desk and, speaking in her wonderful Southern drawl, she talked us through giant scrapbooks filled with examples of her work, and showed us sheaths of fabric samples in varying shades of cream, white, ivory, and the very palest blush.

Seeing the fabric, I began to notice the woman herself. She was elegant with soft blonde hair and high, dramatic cheekbones. Like me, Jeanne was tall; she held herself regally. Seeing someone who carried herself with such confidence intrigued me, and instantly made me feel more at ease.

There was an immediate simpatico between us. At the time, I knew nothing about fashion — I couldn't tell Donatella Versace from Donna Karan. But even though I didn't have the vocabulary, I knew that Jeanne and I spoke the same language. It was one that I'd never heard spoken in my tiny hometown.

[*Imogene + Willie*]

When Jeanne sat down with me to design my dress, she could have sniffed at my desire to go the fairy princess route. Instead, she encouraged me. She showed me ways that she could cut the lace pattern I loved into shapes that would look like petals falling from the tops of my shoulders; it was her idea to weigh each with a clear crystal "tear drop" that I thought looked like morning dew. She loved my impulse of using multiple layers of tulle on the skirt and approved of a bodice inspired by the vintage ballet costumes I used to wear to play dress-up.

I loved my deb dress. That dress was me at 19: sweet and innocent. Wearing it made me feel beautiful and special.

After I took my societal bows, my fairy princess gown was zipped into its plastic garment bag and relegated to my parents' attic with the rest of the dance and party dresses my sisters and I wore during the years we lived under their roof. It was like sealing up a time capsule and walking away.

I always felt like an outsider growing up in my small hometown. As a kid, once I discovered how to use the heavy encyclopedia set that my father installed on a low shelf in the living room, I stole the N volume, and would spend hours poring over the New York City entry, with its photos of traffic in Times Square and the chorus line from an early production of *42nd Street*.

New York City was glamorous. Cleveland, Tennessee, was not. I felt strongly that there was something more than what I knew. It wasn't that I was aching to leave right that minute; I wasn't that ambitious back then. I just knew there was something more waiting outside Bradley County.

Not too many years removed from my visit to Jeanne's atelier, the waiting ended with me living in a dingy four-story walkup on the Lower East Side of Manhattan, covering fashion for the *New York Post*. It was a job "a million girls would kill for," as Anne Hathaway's character, an abused *Vogue* assistant, was told in the movie *The Devil Wears Prada*.

I sat on the front rows at Fashion Week in New York, Paris, and Milan. I covered fancy parties like the annual Costume Institute Gala at the Met. I interviewed designers, from Donatella Versace to Donna Karan, Ralph Lauren to Roberto Cavalli, Diane Von Furstenberg to the late, great Bill Blass. I traveled the world to report stories on the paper's dime.

I was at the *Post* for eight years, and virtually all of my work was in some way related to dresses — gowns, specifically. (I even got to wear some of them: Vera Wang dressed me in a bias-cut peach floral silk gown for a party during the Cannes Film Festival one year; the next, Chanel loaned me a dress to wear to an Oscars party.)

Critiquing red carpets was a big part of my job. It was up to me to determine who wore her gown best and who wore hers worst; whose dress choice was a success, whose was a disaster.

I never felt comfortable trashing someone's fashion choice in print, but the *Post* actively encouraged me to be mean. Snark was their specialty, but it made me cringe. (I wanted to throw up when the stylist of *Sopranos* actress Jamie Lynn Sigler told me that her client had cried for hours when I trashed what I thought was an overly-fluffy Pepto pink cocktail dress that the actress had worn to a movie premiere. Ugh.)

From time to time, I couldn't help but wonder how I might have fared if the cotillion dress I designed was being judged.

I thought of Jeanne.

When I moved to Nashville eight years ago, I was way over dresses. Eight years at the *Post* had burned me out on fashion.

I tried to write about other things — music, art, celebrities, real estate. It never felt right. Lucky for me, there was a burgeoning fashion scene in Nashville that embraced a warm, authentic vintage aesthetic that felt natural to me. So, after several years of spinning my wheels, I was back in fashion, as it were.

I was hired to work with Imogene + Willie, a local fashion company that promotes a lifestyle that's very much a blend of the high fashion I grew to appreciate in New York and the homegrown sensibilities of my mother's closet.

Then, in 2010, something unlikely happened. I was consulting for the Frist Center for the Visual Arts in advance of their *Golden Age of Couture* exhibit, a vast collection of the best of mid-20th Century French and British fashion from the likes of Dior, Balenciaga, Schiaparelli, Balmain and Fath, on loan from London's Victoria & Albert Museum. At a party for the exhibit's launch, a friend said she wanted to introduce me to a local designer whom she thought I would enjoy: Jeanne Dudley Smith.

Jeanne hadn't changed a bit in twenty years. Her elegance and molasses delivery were still in tact. I had evolved, of course, but only in ways that made us more compatible when it came to talking about clothes. After a dozen years in the fashion trenches, I could talk to Jeanne in our shared language.

We walked the exhibit together. We talked about Dior's New Look silhouette, the curves that Balenciaga made a signature of his work, and the exquisite handwork that is still being done by the career embroiderers at Lesage.

While Jeanne and I were catching up that night, something hit me. Everyone in the galleries was looking longingly at the gowns behind the glass, wishing that Pierre Balmain or Else Schiaparelli were still around to make up their dream dresses. They longed for the special connection that comes from building something with someone you admire, but I had no such desires.

They had their fashion fantasies. I had mine.

LIBBY CALLAWAY is the former fashion editor of the *New York Post*. Her writing has appeared in *Glamour*, *Travel + Leisure*, *Nylon*, and *Self*.

⇒ THE LIGHT DRAWS THEM OUT ⇐

Written by **J.WES YODER** | **WHEN I WAS A KID** I wanted badly to see an angel. Instead I saw snakes, and in some way they satisfied my want of the unseen world. At least I could have no doubt about whose side they were on. Lucifer had embodied the serpent, and now the whole lot was cursed. Playing, I would come across a long form in the dry grass, and fear would seize me, and the word would ring, Evil. Around this time I heard a very stupid story. Some friends of my parents who lived along the Harpeth River had found an old and massive water moccasin in their living room. An older couple with sweet temperaments, they decided to rebuke the venomous creature in the Name of God, open the doors, and retire to another room. Sure enough, they came back a while later and the snake was gone. But the poor people, they couldn't be certain if it had returned to the river, or gone behind the bookcase. Weeks were spent in fear.

Clinically speaking, I suffer a phobia of snakes. All of the signs are there; a fear out of proportion to threat, a rapid heartbeat, shortness of breath, and the common behaviors of avoidance and flight. But the diagnosis seems an oversimplification, just as it's not really true to say that I hate snakes. My attitudes towards them are tangled, and while I recoil at even a photograph of a snake, I hardly speak of anything with such eagerness and delight. If in my boyish certainty I decided that the correct thing for the older couple to do would have been to go get a hoe, I now find something sad about acting on my fears, and I'd like to think I've killed my last snake.

But back in our subdivision it was all very simple. Me and my friends would be down at the creek with a pack of raw hot dogs, eating some and baiting the rest to fish. Then along the bank we'd see one and get rocks. To kill something that needed killing felt like a passage. We were keeping the neighborhood safe.

Then I had nightmares. In the one I'd be down by the pond and I'd see a snake in the water. Then another in the grass. Soon there were dozens and nowhere to walk. In the other I had one in the bed, staying warm along my leg. I had to keep still. I'd let my dad know when he came to wake me.

As I grew, my fear was also my fascination, and in popularity Spitting Cobras [See Vipers] and Anacondas ranked not far behind the female anatomy in my most frequent consultations with the *World Book Encyclopedia*. I still take it as a source of pride that of the four venomous species native to North America, three are living here in Nashville. Only the nearly friendly looking coral snake is absent, while ours belong to the pit viper family, an ugly bunch with blunt noses, hooded eyes, and triangular heads. They are the copperhead, a shy type who wears a pattern akin to dead leaves, which in our woods pretty much means the pattern of the snake, if not the thing itself, is everywhere. The cottonmouth, or moccasin, who favors muddy streams, the only kind that flow here. And the rattlesnake, the noble one, who even when camouflaged announces his presence, the snake to whom the boy in Faulkner's "The Bear" raises his hand and names Chief, then Grandfather. As a boy here you learn to identify these, and to tell them apart from the milk snakes, rat snakes, bull snakes, king snakes, water snakes, garter snakes, and the other twenty or so non-dangerous species that are just as likely to occur in your ditch. Here we say a place looks "snaky," and we could be talking about a rocky slope, a dead stump, a drainage culvert, a stand of bamboo, an abandoned car, a woodpile, a crawlspace, or an attic. Several times each winter it crosses my mind that one is never more than 20 or 30 feet away, hibernating as they must be above my ceiling or beneath my floor, and listening to my radio.

Maybe Nashville isn't the snakiest place in the world, but there are an awful lot of them, and if you were a child here you have some stories to tell. Either you stepped on one barefoot while playing kick-the-can, or you found yourself swimming with one in your grandmother's pool, or you successfully chased one down with a push mower. Or else a good dog was seriously bit, or one dropped out of a tree into the family canoe, or an uncle, who was revered in your youth for reasons that now make you sad, used to show off by sneaking up on a sunning snake, snatching it by the tail, twirling it like a whip and then cracking it dead on a rock.

While such stories revive dull dinners, the topic is not entirely uniting. The rub comes, of course, when the talk turns to killing. At this point three divisions of humanity are established: those who never

[*Shelby Bottoms*]

kill, those who kill upon verification of the triangular head, and those who kill indiscriminately, even madly. Here I find myself resisting classification, and more and more, I stay silent.

And yet it seems that a generation ago getting rid of unpleasant things was mostly unquestioned. A number of times I've heard audiences ask the writer Rick Bragg what he will do when he retires, and he always says he's going to move back home with his mother, pull a chair up pondside, and shoot snakes. His audiences are older, and delighted.

I've often worried that the tactile reality of a held serpent might be the only thing to untwine my mind's more sinuous idea. But I've never held a snake, and by some twisted association, I've never even held a frog.

So far I've only taken up a kind of haphazard and self-administered psychotherapy, trying to root my fear out at the source. It seems noteworthy that my two most haunting childhood memories involve instances when no actual snake was seen. In the one I am in the gym where we went on Sundays, and it is missionary morning. No account of famine, rape, mutilation, or martyrdom will compare to the horror told by the man from Africa. He woke in a mud hut with a cobra coiled on his chest, staring into his eyes. For a full day it stayed.

Then there was the summer evening when snake catchers came to clean out the infested neighborhood pond. They shone a spotlight on the water and the snakes, many of them moccasins, came like moths. I'd begged my parents to let me go, but this belonged in that category of unwatchable things like *The Exorcist* and *Dirty Dancing*.

The problem with tracing your fears back to a specific instance is obvious. In the case of the missionary, the adult you will decide easily enough that the man was probably a crook, and anyway, you don't go to bed in Africa. But in the case of the night time snake extraction—muddy-black bodies with white mouths hurrying across black water towards a fixed light, enough venom swimming in their blood to kill every child on your cul-de-sac—you can't tell yourself it did not happen. It did happen, there in a subdivision pond in Bellevue in 1986, and anyway you think about it, it's awful.

I've also speculated that the nightmares are merely visitations of snakes I've killed. There have been plenty, and some stand out more than others. When I was 11 I found a big rat snake in the moisture by the garden hose. I told my father I'd take care of it, and he told me not to chop the hose up with the snake, a cautionary phrase that has always stayed with me, and which I now realize is the exact masculine equivalent of my mother's dictum, "Let's not throw the baby out with the bathwater."

Often folks tell me that snakes in dreams are symbolic. They say it suggestively, as if they are talking to someone who's personal growth has been stunted. What's implied is, "Your phobia's not so charming, just look into it, and be done with it." So recently I tried. According to the literature, a dream snake represents a certain unresolved fear. "Yeah," I blurted, "the snake represents a snake."

The other day I was walking around Radnor Lake with a friend, looking up into the branches to rack my memory for some story I was telling, when she put her hand on my shoulder. It was just a touch, but at that I leaped and shouted, "Where is it!" I'm not sure what she found more impressive, my blind intuition or my emasculating reaction. There, a few paces ahead, some harmless varietal was crossing. The rest of the way I was very excited. "The thing is," I said. "In the fall and spring, they go on the move. Hey, have you heard the theory going around about the East Nashville garter snake boom? Word is the '98 tornado caused it. Imagine, a twister full of scrap tin and west Nashville snakes." I spoke this way for half an hour.

What can I make of that excitement? Or of my disappointment every time I identify a snake in my path as non-venomous? Or of my near heartbreak last fall when a man out in the country said, "Nah, you won't find a rattlesnake in that woodpile. They paved the road out there a few years back and nights they all went out there to keep warm. Thump. Thump. They're all gone."

And what of a phobia's symptoms, isn't there something wonderful about shortened breath and a rapid heartbeat, that heightening of sensitivity in which numbness and memory are erased? Faced with a sudden threat (or sudden love) we all become the first man, without recourse history; we don't know what to do. Maybe afterwards I'll have walked away, or maybe I'll have killed, but for an instant everything before and after had vanished. That might even be innocence, and maybe I don't want to cure that.

In regard to the tornado full of snakes, I was loathe to really look into it. In high school I'd seen that tornado forming over Brentwood. An hour later it had touched down on Broadway, hopped the Cumberland, and laid waste to East Nashville. We came with chainsaws the next morning, and they say that's when the gentrification began, that and the garter snake boom. Now online community chat boards have posts of people seeing them "in knots, ten to twenty, rolling around." But the tornado image was too good to be true. Favoring man-made junk piles, the snakes had made mating palaces of the debris. No one was saying they were born here on the wind.

I moved back South a few years ago and bought a house in East Nashville. Soon after I was cooking paella in my fire pit and one charged out from behind a rock, smacked the bottom of the pan, and died stiff on the coals. Well, I thought, of the dozens I've seen already, that's the only death attributable to me. I'm getting over this thing.

Then one morning I went out to work on my fence. I pulled a tarp back from the bags of Quickcrete and found a snake against the house. After the first rush, I decided that this time I wouldn't kill automatically, although I'd go through the process of identification first, just to be certain. And sure enough the head was a simple oval with smooth skin; it was only a garter snake, a black body with two yellow lines. Pleased with my maturing naturalism, I drew a bag back and poured it in my wheelbarrow, and for peace of mind, I wheeled it over a ways. I stood there mixing, reimagining what was behind me, and that's when the second thrill went up my spine, or maybe it was only anger, and I said, "There were two heads there." And so, with shovel already in hand, I went over to look.

And I found them tangled, in the act of intimacy, staring at one another.

The largest litter of garter snakes on record is 98.

What could I do?

Born in Nashville, **J. WES YODER** wrote his first novel, *Carry My Bones*, after several years as a beat reporter for the *Anniston Star*. Ron Rash calls him "one of the South's most important new literary voices."

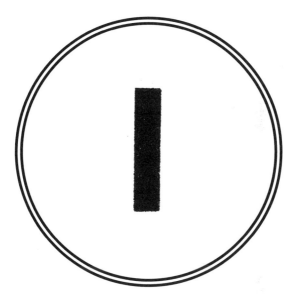

INDEX

≫ INDEX ≪

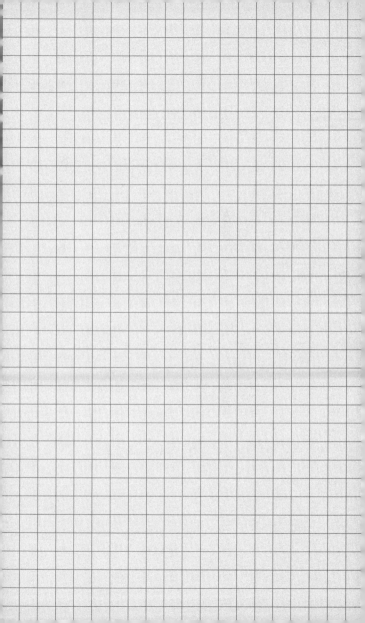